FOURTH ANNUAL CONFERENCE

OF THE

YOUNG PEOPLE'S SOCIETIES

OF

CHRISTIAN ENDEAVOR CONVENTION

HELD AT

Ocean Park, Old Orchard, Maine,

July 8 - 9, 1885.

First Fruits Press
Wilmore, Kentucky
c2015

First Fruits Press
The Academic Open Press of Asbury Theological Seminary
204 N. Lexington Ave., Wilmore, KY 40390
859-858-2236
first.fruits@asburyseminary.edu
asbury.to/firstfruits

FOURTH ANNUAL CONFERENCE

OF THE

YOUNG PEOPLE'S SOCIETY

OF

CHRISTIAN ENDEAVOR,

HELD AT OCEAN PARK, OLD ORCHARD,
MAINE,

JULY 8 AND 9, 1885.

PRINTERS
230
LEWIS & WINSHIP
UNION ST
LYNN MASS

ANNOUNCEMENT.

GENERAL SECRETARY.

At the Annual Convention of the Societies of Christian Endeavor, at Old Orchard, Me., July 8 and 9, 1885, in view of the rapid spread of the movement and the constant calls for information and assistance in forming new societies and carrying on the work, it was voted to put a General Secretary in the field, and the selection of the proper person was left with the Executive Committee. That committee held a meeting in Portland, Me., Aug. 10, and elected Rev. S. Winchester Adriance, of Lowell, Mass., to that position. After long and careful consideration, Mr. Adriance has accepted the appointment and entered upon the work.

The General Secretary is now ready to respond to calls for assistance in extending the work among the churches, and will co-operate in every way possible in the formation of new societies and extending and strengthening those already established. All communications may be addressed to

REV. S. WINCHESTER ADRIANCE.

P. O. Box 1235, Boston, Mass.

UNITED SOCIETY OF CHRISTIAN ENDEAVOR.

A corporation having the above given title was formed at the Annual Convention of the Societies of Christian Endeavor, at Old Orchard, July 8, 1885, under the General Laws of the State of Maine, the object being to bind the different societies closer together in a common interest, and to provide a responsible central organization through which the work of the societies may be carried on, in the way of raising, receiving and paying out money, and giving proper custody for whatever property the society may acquire. The officers of the corporation are substantially the same as those of the convention, the President being W. J. Van Patten, of Burlington. Vt., and the Treasurer, George M. Ward, of Lowell, Mass.

Annual Membership in the United Society is obtained by payment of an annual fee of one dollar. The payment of twenty dollars at one time entitles any member to Life Membership, and relieves him of the annual membership fee.

Membership in the United Society is not limited. Any person, young or old, who is in sympathy with young people and desires to lend his aid and influence to bring them to Christ and help them in their endeavor to form a good Christian character in His service, is earnestly and cordially invited to become a member of the United Society. In this way very many whom age or occupation prevents from membership in local societies may become identified with the general movement and make his interest and influence count for much. Ten annual memberships in each Society of Christian Endeavor thus far organized would provide for nearly all the annual expense thus far authorized, and an increase above that number would enable the society to greatly extend its work. Will not each society take up this matter earnestly, and see if they cannot secure at least ten, and more if possible, members of the United Society, either within their society or among its friends?

Copies of the By-Laws and Certificates of Membership, together with any other desired information concerning the society, may be obtained by addressing George M. Ward, Treasurer, Lowell, Mass., or the General Secretary, Rev. S. W. Adriance, Box 1235, Boston, Mass.

ADDRESS.

The trustees take this means of soliciting correspondence upon all matters that pertain to the method and work of Young People's Societies of Christian Endeavor. When obstacles seem to exist to the formation of societies, it is believed that Mr. Adriance, who is an expert in all these matters and has been unanimously elected on that account, will be able to point out how existing societies have overcome equal or greater difficulties. If any society exists that is not securing the results which these societies — when well worked — uniformly achieve, let us get the organization into effective form. We are not thinking now of money matters, but of the beneficent results of this growing organization. We want to develop an unused factor in Christian work. *It is the cause — the cause* After societies are formed, we are confident they will be moved to aid us in bearing our office expenses for the sake of extending their blessings to others. Someone is responsible for the prompt and regular payment of salary and of printing bills. If this amount is shared among all societies, it will not be burdensome. Where societies bear different names, it is now hoped that for convenience in tabulating results and in extending our literature, they will bear the uniform name. A peculiarity of name does the specific society no additional good, and subtracts just so much from the moral weight of the movement. The conduct of our work is to be reduced by our President and Secretary to strictly business methods, and the counsels of the beloved founder of our society will still be felt in all matters of public policy.

It is confidently expected that there will be a movement this winter all along the line. Correspondence is already flowing in respecting district conferences which we propose to hold all over the land. Our work only needs to be known to be adopted. Our best advertisements are the societies already existing. Anniversary occasions are useful in giving momentum to our work. They should be employed to get our movement before the people. We must relieve our secretary of all financial cares, so that he may give himself to correspondence and to public addresses. It is hoped that ministerial associations and conferences will make a place for the presentation of this cause. Mr. Adriance is open to Sunday engagements, and it is hoped that on Sunday nights he may be engaged for many weeks in advance to speak in behalf of our cause. Anniversaries should be arranged with him very early to avoid conflict of appointment.

COMMENDATION — SAMPLE OF MANY.

The Society of Christian Endeavor has been a great help to us, developing the piety and talents of the young and uniting them in work; also making a center toward which unconverted youth are drawn. It is a most valuable means of good with us.

REV. H. M. GROUT,
Concord, Mass.

MINUTES.

The Fourth Annual Conference of the Young People's Society of Christian Endeavor was held at Ocean Park, Old Orchard, Maine, July 8 and 9, 1885, in pursuance of the announcements of the Executive Committee.

The meeting was called to order at 9.30 of the first day, by the President, Mr. W. H. Pennell, and the first half-hour was spent in devotion, led by Rev. R. W. Brokaw, of Belleville, N. J., who, after reading from the Scriptures, remarked that he hoped the meeting would take on the best characteristics of a Christian Endeavor Prayer Meeting. In the numerous prayers which followed, the presence and guidance of the Holy Spirit was besought for the deliberations to follow.

ORGANIZATION AND BUSINESS.

At 10 o'clock the President again took the chair, and the delegates joined in singing the hymn "To The Work," being accompanied and led by organ, cornet and trombone.

On motion of Rev. S. W. Adriance, of Lowell, Mass., Mr. Clarence W. Hobbs, of Lynn, Mass., was chosen Recording Secretary.

On motion of Rev. F. E. Clark, that a Committee on Credentials be appointed, the President named as such Committee, Messrs. A. L. Winship, of Lynn, Mass., D. F. Small, West Falmouth, Me., Dr. H. T. Carter, Oneida, N. Y., Eli Manchester, New Haven, Conn., and E. II. Shattuck, Lowell, Mass. The Committee immediately went into session in the chapel.

On motion of Rev. J. L. Hill, of Lynn, the programme prepared by the Executive Committee was adopted as the programme of the conference.

On motion of Mr. Hill, of Lynn, it was voted that the paper on Suitable and Sufficient Literature, by Rev. C. A. Stone, of Ravenna, Ohio, which had been sent to the Committee, Mr. Stone not being present at the conference, be read prior to that entitled a Society

Paper, and that the discussion be joined on both together during the last hour of the morning session.

Rev. Mr. Hill for the Executive Committee moved that the persons composing the Business Committee of the last conference be the Business Committee of this, and that the chair fill all vacancies on that committee. The motion prevailed and the Business Committee was subsequently announced as follows: Rev. C. A. Dickenson, Lowell, Mass., Rev. F. E. Clark, Boston, Mass., Mr. C. A. Staples, Portland, Me., Rev. E. Blakeslee of New Haven, Ct., Rev. J. M. Lowden, Portland, Me.

Announcement was made by the chair that badges had been prepared for the delegates, who were requested to provide themselves with the same that they might be distinguished from others in attendance, not delegates. The badges consisted of a piece of white satin ribbon, with the legend "Christian Endeavor, Delegate," printed thereon in red letters. Similar badges were provided for Visitors.

The President then read his annual address, which received marked attention, and on motion of Rev. F. E. Clark, was referred to the Business Committee. The address, together with other papers read at the conference will be found in the appendix.

The report of the Treasurer, Mr. W. J. Van Patten was then read, showing receipts of $294.71 ; expenditures of $236.86, and a balance on hand of $57.85. The report was accepted and ordered printed in the Annual Report.

The Report of the Executive Committee was made by Rev. S. W. Adriance. In addition to the routine business of the year, which had received the attention of the committee, there had been referred to it by the last conference the subjects of a model constitution, and of the advisability of forming a corporation in order that the society might receive, acquire and hold property. A corporation had been formed of which a more extensive report will be made hereafter. A draft of a model constitution had been prepared which he proceeded to read. He said that in preparing such a constitution, difficulty was encountered in the fact that each society is a law unto itself and has its peculiarities of constitution and administration, and there is great difficulty in forming a model constitution that would suit all. The committee recommended that the constitution which should be adopted by this conference be printed, and the variations and peculiarities incident to different societies be added thereto in the form of suggestions.

The discussion which followed was participated in by Rev. Messrs. Dickenson, Brokaw, Hall, Hill and Clarke, and Dr. Hawes of Burlington, Vt., and Mr. Hubbard of Rochester, N. Y., after which the report went to the Business Committee.

The paper on Suitable and Sufficient Literature was read by Mr. C. A. Hight of Williston Society, Portland, Me. The importance of a supply of good literature in the promotion of Christian work and developement of christian character was presented in a thoughtful and interesting manner. Mr. C. W. Hobbs of Lynn, Mass., followed with a paper entitled "A Society Paper." The need of a paper devoted to the interests of the Society was dwelt upon, the subject being considered under the heads: Why do we need a society paper? What kind of a paper do we want, and How may we have it? The writer insisted upon the desirability of an independent sheet as opposed to a department in some religious paper now published, and the necessity of rallying heartily to the support of such a paper.

The discussion following the paper was very lively and participated in by a large number, Bros. Cushing of Montreal, Hall of Auburn, Hill of Lynn, Grose of Poughkeepsie, and Clark of Somerville, speaking in favor of having an independent paper. Mr. Shumway of Melrose presented figures showing the cost of publishing such a paper as would be required, and thought the societies were not ready to undertake the enterprise this year, though he favored ultimately having a paper all our own.

Rev. Mr. Dickenson thought that in fairness to the publishers of the Golden Rule, (a religious paper published in Boston) it should be stated that they had offered to print a certain amount of matter each week relating to the work of the societies, if it could in return be made the official paper of the movement, and to make its terms one dollar a year to members of the societies, and to clubs of ten, ninety cents. Rev. F. E. Clark being asked his opinion said he had been approached by several parties in the interests of the Golden Rule, but as yet he had not made up his mind. Rev. Mr. Grose thought the offer of the Golden Rule a generous, and in one sense a captivating one, but in our work in the world at large a paper of our own would better subserve our aims. The discussion was continued till 12.20, when the morning session was closed by singing the Doxology.

WEDNESDAY AFTERNOON.

A praise meeting conducted by Rev. J. M. Lowden of Portland, preceded the general session of the convention, which was called to order at 2.20 by the President, and prayer was offered by Rev. J. J. Hall of Auburn. The Committee on Credentials made a partial report which showed 161 delegates present, representing 61 societies.

Rev. Mr. Clark, from the Business Committee reported reference to committees of subjects as follows:

Committee on the paper of Mr. Hobbs on a Society Paper: Mr. W. J. Van Patten, Rev. C. A. Dickenson, Rev. H. B. Grose, Mr. F. P. Shumway, Jr., Mr. W. S. Clarke, of Somerville.

Committee to Nominate Officers for the Ensuing Year: Rev. J. L. Hill, Rev. S. W. Adriance, Rev. J. M. Lowden, Mr. W. D. Hubbard, Mr. Frank Knapp.

Committee on the Suggestion of the President in regard to State Conferences: Rev. R. W. Brokaw, Rev. J. J. Hall, Rev. N. Boynton, Mr. Geo. N. Ward, Mr. Wm. Shaw.

The regular order of the afternoon was then taken up, the first subject being presented by Mr. F. P. Shumway, Jr.. of Melrose, Mass., in a paper entitled " Qualifications for Active Membership." The writer gave a consensus of opinion upon the subject by means of extracts from a large number of letters received by him. The weight of opinion being that in a matter so intimately connected with the life of the society, the standard of qualification for membership should be kept high.

The subject of Associate Membership was presented in an able paper by Rev. S. W. Adriance, of Lowell, Mass., which is printed entire in the appendix.

The Duties of the President were discussed by Mr. Wm. Shaw, Jr., of So. Boston, showing that by a right use of the opportunities offered by his position, the President may and should exercise great influence in the life of the society.

Interesting remarks on the subject of the paper were made by Bros. Shaw, of Burlington, and Manchester, of New Haven.

Miss M. Alice Metcalf, of the Williston Society, Portland, Me., read an interesting paper on the duties of the Secretary, which was full of valuable suggestions in regard to keeping both the business and membership record. She exhibited the records of the Williston Society, as kept by herself, and at the conclusion of the paper, on motion of Rev. J. L. Hill, Miss Metcalf was requested to prepare specimen pages of a model Secretary's book for insertion in the minutes. This specimen will be found in the appendix.

The audience then rose and sang three verses of "Stand up for Jesus," after which the discussion on the subject of " Christian Growth as related to practical Christian Life," was opened by Rev. E. Blakeslee, of New Haven, followed by Rev. R. W. Brokaw, of Belleville, N. J., and Rev. Dr. Hawes, of Burlington, Vt. The papers were all of great interest, and occupied the remainder of the afternoon.

WEDNESDAY EVENING.

While the convention was gathering a service of song was held, which was generally participated in. At 7.30 Bro. W. J. Van Patten made a statement regarding the corporation which had been formed, which was supplemented by remarks by Rev. J. L. Hill. This corporation, formed under the laws of the state of Maine, is now in existence, and the delegates were invited to become charter members thereof, the only condition of membership being that the person becoming a member should also be a member of some Evangelical church, in good standing, and pay a membership fee of one dollar annually. Life memberships may be purchased at twenty dollars. In response to the invitation, seventy names were handed in, in about fifteen minutes, and others during the continuation of the conference.

At 7.50, the General Secretary, Jas. W. Stevenson, began to read his report, but owing to the lateness of the hour, he was obliged to curtail the reading to give place to Rev. Alex. McKenzie, of Cambridge, Mass., who gave an earnest address to young men on their aim in life. A large audience had by this time gathered. The address was an able and interesting effort and received marked attention. At its close the meeting was dismissed, Rev. C. A. Dickenson pronouncing the benediction.

THURSDAY MORNING.

The eight o'clock prayer meeting was led by Rev. R. G. Woodbridge, of Iowa, which was followed by a song service led by Bro. A. A. Arnold of Providence, R. I.

At 9 o'clock, Rev. R. W. Brokaw, from the committee on the Suggestion of the President regarding State Conferences, made the following report:

REPORT OF COMMITTEE ON THE ADVISABILITY OF RECOMMENDING STATE CONFERENCES.

Your committee would respectfully report that the suggestion of Mr. Pennell, our President, in regard to holding state conventions of the Association of Christian Endeavor, seems to them to be a good one. There are, however, a few things to be taken into consideration, before recommending that it be put into practice. One of these is the necessary expense which they will cause. Another is the possibility of their formulating questions to be answered and schemes to be discussed, and "nuts to be cracked" at the annual conferences which such conferences *will* not have the time and *may* not have the inclination to deal with. And still another is the possibility of their detracting somewhat from the interest which now centers in the general annual conference.

Whether with these and other difficulties which may arise, this conference will deem it wise to recommend state conventions or not, your committee is not able to say, of course. They are perfectly willing to leave the settlement of this matter with them. Nevertheless we are inclined to think, in spite of all obstacles, such conferences are a possibility, if not at present, some time in the near future, and should help our work all along the line.

We therefore offer the following resolutions:

1. *Be it resolved* that in every state, where there are more than two societies of Christian Endeavor, this conference recommends that there be an annual state convention; that this convention occur sometime during the autumn or winter months, and that it remain in session not longer than one day.

2. *Be it resolved* that each state convention shall send one delegate to represent that state as a delegate at large.

3. *Be it resolved* that this change in regard to our present method of sending delegates to the *annual* conference shall be the *only* one made by the introduction of state conferences to the ways now in vogue for carrying forward the work of the society of Christian Endeavor.

The report was adopted.

Mr. Van Patten, from the committee on a society paper, made the following report:

REPORT OF COMMITTEE ON A SOCIETY PAPER.

The committee on the Paper would report that in their opinion, a paper, to be the organ and distinct representative of this society, is very greatly needed, and should be established at the earliest practicable moment. They are not, however, prepared to recommend its immediate establishment. Estimates showing that such a paper as would be desirable, would require a financial guarantee of at least one thousand dollars for the first year; and it not being clear that we shall be able to put a paid secretary in the field, and at the same time furnish this needed support, we would therefore recommend that the matter be referred to the Board of Trustees, with power to act; and that if the Board do not decide to establish the paper at once, they avail themselves of the generous offer of the Golden Rule—to use its columns to give such information regarding the Society of Christian Endeavor, as the Board of Trustees may deem best.

If a Secretary be employed, we would recommend that he issue, at regular times, either quarterly or more frequently, a bulletin, giving a synopsis of the work, and recommendations for its more effective prosecution by the local societies.

Rev. Dr. Westwood, of Auburn, Me., moved to amend the report by striking out the clause which gives the Board of Trustees " power to act," and to insert " that they be instructed to report to the next convention." This motion was opposed by Rev. Messrs. Blakeslee and Pope, and Messrs. Cushing, of Montreal, and Van Patten; after which, on suggestion of Mr. Pope, Dr. Westwood withdrew his amendment, remarking that he always obeyed the mandates of the Pope, and the report was adopted as made.

Rev. Mr. Clark referring to the model constitution, asked authority for the executive committee to have the model constitution printed with such amendments as they may deem necessary.

Mr. Hill of Lynn asked that the variations thereto, in use in different places be printed in the same connection as addenda, for use as suggestions, etc.

The model constitution was again read, and also the variations alluded to by Bro. Adriance, whereupon the whole matter was referred to Executive Committee, with power.

Rev. J. L. Hill, from the Committee on Nominations, made a report.

He referred to the tacit understanding, held since the beginning, that there should be rotation in office, and before any new nominations were made he desired for the committee, and he felt sure he should but voice the sentiments of the convention, to make acknowledgement of the services of President Pennell during his term of office. He then offered the following:

Resolved, That the thanks of the societies of Christian Endeavor in convention assembled are richly due and are hereby tendered to our retiring President, Mr. W. H. Pennell, for his wise, strenuous, generous and untiring labor in our behalf. We desire to make recognition of our feeling that he has always honored us by representing us, and that the societies whose well-being he has promoted are the monuments of his unselfish and unflagging efforts during his three years of service.

The motion was warmly seconded by Bro. F. E. Clark, who spoke from his personal knowledge as associate with Mr. Pennell on the Executive Committee; by Bro. J. M. Lowden, who asked leave to interpolate an Amen, after the fashion of the Baptist brethren, and by Bro. J. W. Stevenson, who made ackowledgement of the aid which Mr. Pennell had always given him in his department of the work.

As a further acknowledgement of the service which Mr. Pennell had rendered the cause, Mr. Hill moved that he be requested to preside during the continuance of this convention.

Both the resolution and motion were adopted by a rising vote.

Mr. Pennell made feeling acknowledgement of the testimonial.

Mr. Hill from the Nominating Committee then made a partial report, provision being asked to reserve the list of Vice Presidents to be further revised, the idea being to have the Vice Presidents so arranged that each should act as a State President. The list of officers reported were:

President. W. J. VAN PATTEN, Burlington, Vt.

Secretary. W. J. STEVENSON, Portland, Me.

Treasurer. GEORGE N. WARD, Lowell, Mass.

Executive Committee. Rev. F. E. CLARKE, South Boston, Mass.; Rev. C. A. DICKENSON, Lowell, Mass.; Rev. J. L. HILL, Lynn, Mass.; W. H. PENNELL, Portland, Me.; Rev. J. M. LOWDEN, Portland, Me..; Rev. S. W. ADRIANCE, Lowell, Mass.; Rev. R. W. BROKAW, Belleville N. J.; Rev. H. B. GROSE, Poughkeepsie, N. Y.

On motion of Rev. F. E. Clark, the Recording Secretary was directed to cast a ballot in behalf of the Convention for the officers above named, which was done.

The new President was then invited to a seat upon the platform, and was received with loud applause. He responded briefly, pledging himself to the work to the extent of his ability. He said he could not hope to fill the place of Mr. Pennell, but trusted he should have the support and prayers of the members of the Convention.

Rev. F. E. Clark spoke of the qualifications of the new President as evinced by his works and gifts in the past; and Dr. Hawes, of Burlington, President Van Patten's pastor, spoke of his feeling of satisfaction and his sense of reflected glory that the choice for so important an officer should have fallen on one of his flock.

Rev. Dr. Westwood invoked the blessing of God on the newly elected officers.

The regular discussions were taken up and Rev. F. E. Clark read a paper on " Need of a General Secretary." The subject was presented in a clear and forcible manner.

Rev. R. W. Brokaw warmly seconded the recommendations of of Mr. Clark, and stated that rather than not have a General Secretary appointed he for his Society would become responsible for $50 toward his expenses.

Bro. Shaw, of So. Boston, said his Society would be responsible for the second $50.

Rev. Mr. Boynton, of Haverhill, pledged his Society for the third $50.

Dr. Hawes, of Burlington, Vt., said his Society would come forward with the fourth $50.

Bros. Manchester, of New Haven, and D. P. Stacy, of Lowell, said their Societies would not be behind with their support.

Rev. Mr. Pope wished that some one would speak on the other side of the question. He also remarked that some one has been doing the work of a Secretary who has not been paid. He thought recognition of this fact should be made, but if there was anything to be said on the other side he would like to hear it. The whole matter was referred to the Business Committee.

Mr. W. J. Van Patten read a paper on "A Business View of Ways and Means," which was followed by a paper prepared by J. T. Alling, of Rochester, N. Y., read by Mr. Hubbard of the same place. The title of the paper was " How to Promote Faithfulness to the Prayer Meeting Pledge," Remarks upon this paper were made by several delegates, special reference being made to the growing degree of participation by ladies in the prayer meetings.

Mr. Shumway, of Melrose, Mass., asked for advice, so many of the members of his Society profess inability to take part in the meeting, though giving most pronounced daily evidence of deep and fervent piety. The case of one young lady was cited who after weeks of attendance with the intention of taking part, fainted while attempting to repeat a verse of the Scripture.

Rev. Mr. Brokaw believed the rule should be insisted on. While girls can chatter so volubly on every nameable topic when alone, so much diffidence in public, savors of sham modesty.

"A paper entitled, " Our Younger Members," by Rev. J. J. Hall, Auburn, Me., was a loving token of appreciation of the little ones in Christ. " Welcome the boys and girls into the society," said the Reverend gentleman, " even if they cannot keep so still and be as decorous as the older ones."

Bro. J. W. Stevenson endorsed all Mr. Hall had said, but would go further and have children on many of the committees. Bro. Shumway would go still further and give them particular work to do. He was followed by Miss Stevens, of Conway, Mass., who spoke of the part the children had taken in their Society.

Prayer was offered by Rev. Mr. Marsh, of Woodfords, Me., after which Mr. A. L. Winship from the Committee on Credentials, made a final report, showing 209 delegates present representing 82 Societies.

The following committees were appointed :

On Mr. Clark's Paper, "Need of a General Secretary," Rev. J. L. Hill, Dr. E. Hawes, Rev. C. H. Pope, Rev. N. Boynton, Mr. C. Cushing, Rev. Mr. Dutton.

On Mr. Van Patten's Paper on Ways and Means, Rev. S. W. Adriance. Rev. C. H. Westwood, Rev. L. H. Hallock, Mr. D. P. Stacy, Mr. Geo. P. Graff, Rev. T. G. Clark.

Adjourned to 2 P. M.

AFTERNOON.

A spirited service of song was held at 2 P. M., led by A. A. Arnold. When the convention was finally called to order, Mr. Wood, of Syracuse, on behalf of the Societies in New York, invited the Executive Committee to turn its gaze westward when selecting a place for next year's meeting.

The first paper of the afternoon, entitled '' The Experience Meeting," was read by Rev. C. H. Pope, of Farmington. The paper bristled with good points, the speaker urging that too many testimonies are mere set phrases and are not expression of personal experience or personal need, and are closely allied to cant. Let the words spoken in the experience meeting be the expression of a real living experience. Rather than fall into the use of set, meaningless phrases the young christian had better not speak at all. He set little value on testimonies which had not their origin in earnest christian living.

An interesting discussion followed, which the President had to cut short, the time having arrived for the next paper on '' The future of the Y. P. S. C. E., by Rev. J. L. Hill, of Lynn, Mass. This paper was very interesting and well delivered, the closest attention of the audience being claimed at the outset and held throughout. The possibilities of wide success and great development, and also of failure were dwelt upon, and the remedy for possible errors into which the Societies may fall, pointed out.

In answer to the call for a report of the Committee on General Secretary, Mr. Hill, as chairman of that Committee, stated that while our imperative need of a general secretary was unquestioned, all agreed that the position could not be filled by a second-rate man, and that a man possessing the ability the position requires should command a salary of $1,500.00.

This being true, of course the Committee could not proceed further without receiving some assurance from the societies that the needful salary would be provided.

There had already been pledged by individual societies some $200.00, with the expectation that others would add sufficient to make the sum appreciable. Could this amount be raised to $500.00, the Committee would feel authorized to proceed.

Can't we, said Mr. Hill earnestly, just as an expression of our interest in this project, make the amount so generously pledged $500.00 ; now who would like, by a gift of $50.00, to express his faith in the work? At once a response came from a delegate of the Second Parish, Portland, who pledged $50.00 in the name of his society. Others quickly followed, the enthusiasm spreading, and in an incredibly short time the Secretary's figures showed that $570.00 had been subscribed.

Let us now sing, said Mr. Hill, "I love Thy Kingdom, Lord," but there was a protest, and in a few moments more $620.00 had been secured. Why not make it eight hundred? asked Mr. Hill, enthusiastically, and after every hundred subscribed we will sing a verse of this hymn, singing the first verse now. The words were taken up heartily and sung to the tune of Shirland.

Now what society will give $25.00 of the next hundred, Mr. Hill asked; The appeal met a ready response, one delegate pledging $50.00, saying he had had his doubts about our getting a general secretary, but if it was to be done he wanted a hand in it. Mr. Hill expressed a strong desire to shake hands with that man. This completing the hundred, the leader gave out "I love Thy Church, O God," and this time the words found expression in Hebron's well-known strain.

Ninety-five dollars of the next hundred was speedily pledged, and then there was a momentary pause. .Who will give five dollars to make this a hundred, Mr. Hill asked, and Miss Grace Perry, of Williamstown, pledged the amount amid cheers.

The next verse of the hymn being called for it was taken up to the tune of Boylston, for the sake of a change.

Mr. Hill then proposed making the amount a thousand, calling for small pledges, and the sum named being quickly reached and passed, Rev. Mr. Dickenson, rising, said his society would give the last $50 of the twelfth hundred.

The enthusiasm became intense; one delegate would pledge $50 if his neighbor would pledge the same; his neighbor did not like to be outdone.

Rev. Mr. Boynton, of Haverhill, pledged $5.00 for his boy of 3 years, and $5.00 for his girl 4 weeks old.

There lacked at last just $10.00 of the $1200. "Our society will give that," said a delegate from the Central Church, Fall River, and from many thankful hearts there swelled the grand old Doxology, "Praise God, from whom all blessings flow."

This was the most interesting half-hour of the Conference. The proposition to raise the fund for the General Secretary was a complete surprise to the Convention as well as to the Committee, the matter having been discussed by them and thought not to be feasible. The plan of raising the money was adopted by Mr. Hill on the spur of the moment, and met with an equally spontaneous reception by those present.

On motion of Rev. R. W. Brokaw, the report of the Committee was accepted and the thanks of the Convention extended to Mr. Hill.

Following is a list of the subscribers.

SUBSCRIPTIONS FOR GENERAL SECRETARY.

Society in Second Parish, Portland	$50
" Central Presbyterian Church, Rochester, N. Y.	50
" North Church, Lynn	50
" Phillips Church, So. Boston	50
" Church, Burlington, Vt.	50
" Church, Haverhill.	50
" Calvary Congregational Church, Montreal	20
" Williston Church, Portland	50
" Church, Grafton, Mass.	15
" Church, Great Falls, N. H.	25
" Humphrey Street Congregational Church, New Haven, Conn.	50
" Second Congregational Church, Woodfords, Me	15
" Prospect Hill Church, Somerville Mass.	15
" Winthrop Church, Charlestown	15
" Third Congregational Church, Burlington, Vt.	25
" Pilgrim Church, St. Louis, Mo.	15
" No. Avenue Church, Cambridge, Mass.	25
" Second Church, Fair Haven.	10
" Union Church, Ballardvale, Mass.	10
" Howard Avenue Church, New Haven	10
" First Baptist Church, Poughkeepsie, N. Y.	15
" Free Baptist Church, Portland, Me.	10
" Cumberland Centre, Me.	15
" Second Congregational Church, West Newton	50
" Union Church, Providence	25
" Immanuel Church, Boston	25
" Lafayette Church, Buffalo	20
" Free Baptist	10
" Second Church, Dorchester	15
" Congregational Church, Melrose	10
" High St. Church, Auburn, Me.	10
" Ashfield, Mass.	5
" West Congregational Church, Portland	10
" Newton Highlands.	5
" Free St. Baptist Church, Portland, Me.	10
" St. Lawrence St. Church, Portland, Me	10
" Congregational Church, Essex, Mass.	10

Amount carried forward, $855

Amount brought forward,		$855
Society in	Second Congregational Church, Holyoke	50
"	Vergennes, Vt.	10
"	So. Church, St. Johnsbury	10
	Walnut Ave. Church, Roxbury, Mass	25
	Conway, Mass.	5
"	Belleville, N. J.	10
"	Concord, Mass.	5
"	Bucksport, Me.	5
"	Allen Evangelical Church, Dedham, Mass.	10
"	Pilgrim Church, St. Louis. (Add.)	10
"	Warren Church, Cumberland Mills	10
"	First Baptist Church, Portland	10
"	Pine St. Church, Portland	10
"	First Presbyterian Church, Oneida, N. Y.	25
"	Central Church, Fall River	10
"	Kirk St. Church, Lowell, Mass.	50
Mrs. Glidden, Cumberland Mills, Me.		10
F. E. Clark, Boston		10
Mary A. Perkins, Portland, Me.		10
W. J. Van Patten, Burlington, Vt.		25
Miss Grace Perry, Williamstown, Mass.		5
Rev. —— Clarke, Gloucester		10
Rev. Mr. Boynton for child 3 years		5
" " " 4 weeks		5
Miss Nellie Maudant, Lynn		5
R. E. Woodbridge, Osage, Iowa		5
Rev. J. M. Dutton		10
		$1,210

Dr. Westwood from the Committee on Mr. Van Patten's paper made the following report:

REPORT OF THE COMMITTEE ON WAYS AND MEANS.

The Committee on Ways and Means would respectfully report:

We have had under careful consideration the paper submitted by Mr. Van Patten on " A Business View of Ways and Means," and find certain valuable suggestions that if carried out might render our Societies more efficient, which suggestions we would embody in the following resolutions:

Resolved, That in view of the increased expense of furnishing documents relating to the work of our Association, a price sufficient to cover the necessary cost of printing and forwarding the same should be charged for the larger and more expensive pamphlets.

Resolved, That we would recommend the holding of a State and local Conferences under the lively management of lively members, for the purpose of creating a more general interest in the work of our Societies.

Resolved, That our Executive Committee be instructed to arrange as far as may be possible for a proper representation of our Society before the Conferences, Associations, Synods, Conventions, and other ecclesiastical bodies of our country, that reports of the practical efficiency of our Societies may be clearly and fully presented.

Resolved, That among the methods whereby the money for meeting our expenses may be met, we would recommend:

1. An annual assessment upon the several Societies.
2. Appeals to individual Christians for donations.
3. An effort to induce our churches to place our Society work among the objects of Christian benevolence.
4. Membership fees.

Your Committee would leave the working out of the details suggested in these resolutions to the Executive Committee of the Society. We would call upon the various Associations to forward to the Secretary the names of all persons to whom appeals for financial assistance may be presented.

We have not deemed it necessary to say anything concerning the publication of a paper and the employment of a General Secretary as these matters have been referred to a special Committee.

The report of the Committee was accepted and adopted.

Owing to the lateness of the hour the papers of Rev. J. M. Lowden and Rev. C. A. Dickenson were, on motion of those gentlemen, passed over, it being voted, on motion of Mr. Dutton, that these gentlemen be requested to prepare their papers for publication.

The question box was then opened by Rev. F. E. Clark.

A heavy thunder shower approaching, a portion of the audience left the temple for their hotels. Those who remained gathered closer about the desk, and enjoyed the exercises very much. About forty questions were asked, the occasion being improved by many to get light upon the difficult points which had arisen in their experience in their societies.

Among the questions asked were the following:

" What shall be done with active members who do not take part in the prayer meetings?" *Answer*—" Be patient, and work them for all they are worth."

" How shall we interest the younger members in missions?" *Answer*—" By giving them mission work to do at home."

" If we cannot give an experience in a meeting that will be helpful, is it best to give any at all?" *Answer.* — " Any real experience of God's dealings with his children is helpful." " Are there any Societies among the colored people?" *Answer.*—" Not at present."

" What can be done to cause the members to feel the absolute necessity of attending the meetings, or sending an excuse when obliged

to be absent?"   *Answer.* — "Perhaps by educating the conscience."
"In how many Societies do the ladies lead the meetings?'   *Answer.* — "In most."
"How can the younger members be drawn out to take part in the regular meetings?"   *Answer.* — "By personal efforts on the part of the pastor and older members." "What will you do with active members who have lapsed from membership."   *Answer.* — "He should be labored with by the pastor."   "If a person on the associate list is known to have bad habits, would you cut him off?"   "If he refuses to reform, yes."

"Should a Christian be permitted to join a Society as an associate member when he is not willing to do what is required of an active member?"

The discussion on this question developed a difference of opinion and no final answer was given.

Rev. R. W. Brokaw, who was compelled to go home on the evening train bade his friends in the Convention "good-bye," and on request led in prayer.

Adjourned till evening.

THURSDAY EVENING.

The Conference reassembled at 7.30.   Prayer by Rev. L. H. Hallock.

The Committee on Nominations reported the following list of Vice Presidents :

New York . . . . Rev. T. W. HOPKINS, Rochester.
Iowa . . . . Rev. C. A. TOWLE, Montecello.
Connecticut . . . . Rev. E. BLAKESLEE, New Haven.
New Jersey . . . . Rev. B. S. EVERETT, Jamesburg.
Massachusetts . . . . Rev. Dr. ALEXANDER MCKENZIE, Cambridge.
Canada . . . . Bro. CHARLES CUSHING, Montreal.
Indiana   . . . . *. . . .   . Rev. W. J. DARBY, Evansville.
Rhode Island . . .   . Bro. A. A. ARNOLD, Providence.
Vermont . . . . Bro. GEORGE H. PERKINS, Burlington.
Missouri . . . . Rev. Dr. C. L. GOODELL, St. Louis.
Maine   . . . . Rev. J. J. HALL, Auburn.

There being some time remaining the paper entitled, "Fellowship among Societies," was read by Rev. J. M. Lowden of Portland.

Dr. Albert W. Burnham, of Lowell, was chosen Auditor.

Then followed an address by Rev. O. P. Gifford, D. D., of Boston. The speaker occupied about three-fourths of an hour.

Prayer was offered by C. A. Dickinson.

The following vote was unanimously adopted :

Voted, To send a cordial vote of thanks to the Ocean Park Association for their great kindness in giving the Conference the use of their Temple, its many conveniences and appliances.

All joined in singing "Blest be the tie that binds."

The Benediction was pronounced by Rev. F. E. Clark.

Adjourned *sine die.*

SECRETARY'S REPORT.

It is only a little over eight months since some of us met at Kirk St. Church, Lowell, and enjoyed the hospitality of that most cordial people Does the delightful and inspiring christian fellowship of that gathering linger in our memories, with stimulating influence, has the enthusiasm we carried from it kindled eager and delightful anticipation in the minds and hearts of those who gather with us here for the first time?

Believing that such is the case, are our enthusiasm and anticipation wedded to a purpose? Have we come here with fixed resolve, a renewed zeal for our work ; have we come with endeavor, "christian endeavor?" It is he who endeavors that reaches the summit of the mountain, and who is rewarded by the wondrous beauty of the landscape that stretches out before and around him.

This must be an endeavor conference, filled with the endeavor spirit, if it would arouse endeavor societies to faithfulness, zeal and spiritual power.

And now let us see if there is anything in the reports coming to us that will inspire new courage, impart new strength, and implant a lofty, holy purpose of christian endeavor for the months before us.

At our last conference it was stated that one word, " progress," would represent the report in condensed form ; the same is true but in greater measure for the present.

Bear in mind the fact that the last report covered a period of fifteen and a half months, while the present covers only eight and a half; then by comparing the figures of the following schedule we shall gain some knowledge of the favor into which our organization is growing and the advance it is making.

Year.	No. Societies.	Active Members	Associate Members.	Total Members.	Church Members.	United with Church.
1885 . .	253	10958	3934	14892	8443	1121
1884 . .	156	6566	2339	8905	4971	623
Gain . .	97	4392	1595	5987	3472	499

Seventy-seven of the Societies gained have been organized since last Conference ; the other twenty had been organized but not reported, which indicates the fact that there are very many Societies throughout the land and neighboring Dominion of which we have never heard.

Of the 5987 total membership gained, 918 have been gained by additions to Societies previously reported, this represents a part of the work of the Societies. A word here with regard to losses and gains. While the schedule reveals that each of the States has made a net gain, it will also show that there have been some losses ; and the schedule of Societies will set forth the fact that one or two Societies have met with heavy losses. The loss of associate where there is a gain of active members will show probably merely an apparent loss, the associates having become active, but the loss of active members is more serious. The fact that such losses have occurred should rouse the proper committees to active, earnest work to prevent such by faithful work with the careless ones, and by renewed effort to increase the membership, not for the sake of a large membership and a good record at the Conference, but for the sake of the Divine Master and for the glory and strength of His kingdom.

The prominent feature of the reports as they have come to us is the frequent mention of revivals and conversions, and in this connection it is very gratifying and encouraging to hear the many words of commendation expressed by the pastors. Some Societies have been organized as a necessity because of these revivals. It would be presumption to claim that these revivals and many conversions are due to the Societies of Christian Endeavor; but we do know that they have shared in the work and in the blessing and that at least some have been brought into the kingdom of God by their instrumentality.

The following are the reports of some of the Societies, typical ones have been selected that we may not be wearied by repetition. They will be found at once suggestive, encouraging and worthy of imitation.

Society at Berkley, Cal., reports: "Good attendance during the year," and gives the following as the method of its work. "The first half hour at each meeting is devoted to expositions of a Bible Catechism and answering questions from a question drawer. The Society then breaks up into sections, each having a section leader, and holding half hour prayer meetings by themselves."

Society at St. John, N. B., Germain Street Baptist, reports: " Society is now in a better condition than ever before, * * * each member feels individual responsibility, * * * our committees are in first-class working order. * * * Contributions to the Missionary Fund are such that we are now paying half the necessary money for the support of a native preacher in India." This report is of peculiar interest when compared with its report of last year, viz: " Considerable negligence on the part of members," but " they pledged themselves to be more diligent, so that we look for greater results and feel encouraged at the prospect." Here was an honest pledge faithfully redeemed.

Society at Kensington, Conn., reports: Having " undertaken the raising of forty dollars for Whitman College, Washington Territory."

Society at New Haven, Conn., Humphrey Street Church, reports: " Continuous religious interest, not spasmodic; unaffected by heat or cold, still continues."

Society at Thompsonville, Conn., First Presbyterian Church reports: "Although young we can give a good report: 1st. Great improvement in the church socially. 2nd. Many workers developed. 3d. General reconsecration of all active members. 4th. Very earnest and delightful devotional meeting, precious souls saved, to God be all the glory."

Society at West Haven, Conn., reports: "We have raised by festivals, etc. a little over $400, with this carpeted our lecture room, placed a new platform and pulpit in the church and purchased a piano, upon which we have paid $146. Out Missionary Committee have made a canvass of the town and prepared a directory giving where each person attended church (if at all) and whether the children attended S. S. or not. They have carefully noted cases of removal and new comers: thus giving our Pastor valuable aid and forming a basis upon which to conduct their work.

Society at Evansville, Ind., reports through the Pastor, Rev. W. J. Darby as follows: Our society is doing excellent work. "Mr. Darby delivered a series of lectures in Lebanon, Tenn., and in speaking on the work among the young people, he gave it as his experience, after a year's trial, that the Y. P. S. C. E. is the best thing for young people he had ever seen.

Society at Montecello, Iowa, reports: "Out of this work (the work of Y. P. S. C. E.) have grown other meetings, a boy's and young men's praying circle at the pastor's study, a young ladies' and girls' praying circle and a children's meeting. The circles have been a special means of grace to our younger and more timid members, as they were free to speak and lead in prayer, when they felt they could not in the larger meeting."

Society at Tabor, Iowa, reports through Pastor, Rev. J. W. Cowan: "Our society is substantially a children's society. It has been a year of steady, quiet work, and a growing feeling of wonder how we ever got along without the S. C. E. Our society of C. E. meetings are the best of all our prayer meetings."

Society at El Dorado, Kan., reports: "Three of the young men in giving their experience said that the "Picket" (name of the society) meeting had been the chief instrument in leading them to the Savior."

Society at Cornish, Me., reports through pastor, Rev. Z. Crowell, "It is the interesting meetings we have. It has been a great blessing to our young people."

Society at Cumberland Centre, Me., reports: "Before January 1st small meetings and few to take part. We were well nigh disheartened, but with the 'Week of Prayer' and the meetings which followed, there came the blessed assurance that the Lord was with us and many precious souls were 'turned from darkness to light,' twenty-nine of whom have become members of our Society."

Society at Cumberland Mills, Me., reports: "A blessed revival toward which the Young People's Society did its part."

Society at Charlestown, Mass., reports: "The Society adopted the plan of forming the Society into bands as recommended at the last Conference. It is doing good work among the members."

Society at Essex, Mass., reports: "That it started in weakness, some almost repenting the move." It started with nine active members. "Soon after our meetings increased in members and interest. All through the winter and spring we received additions to our active membership. Since then nearly all have joined the church. There has been no excitement but a steady interest. God has blessed the young of this community through the work of this Society."

Society at Franklin, Mass., reports: "Miss Mary Daniels, one of our active members, is going as a missionary to Harpoot, Turkey."

Society at Haverhill, Mass., West Congregational church, report by pastor, Rev. J. N. Lowell: "Increased interest and efficiency."

Society at Holyoke, Mass., "Raised about $450 for a piano fund."

Society at Lowell, Mass., French Protestant Church, reports: "Most of the members are converts from Romanism. Our Society is doing well. It has already produced good results. Our young people show a great interest in the service of God."

Society at Lynn, Mass., North Congregational Church, reports: "The holding of meetings, in other churches for the purpose of forming Societies similar to our own, has been a distinctive feature of the year's work. An increase of working power among the members has been apparent."

Society at Melrose, Mass., reports: "A steady growth into full Christian manhood among our active members, and an appreciation of and readiness to do all Christian work." Our Society has been the means, through its officers, of starting five other Eastern Societies the past year. One by correspondence in California.

Society at Shelburn Falls, Mass., reports by pastor, Rev. J. H. Hoffman: "A number of conversions, some twenty-five during the winter. Visits to other Societies."

Society at Somerville, Mass., Prospect Hill, reports: "This Society seems to meet a long felt want in our church in banding our young people together for more active Christian work."

Society at Minneapolis, Minn., reports through pastor, Rev. H. C. Hovey, D. D.: "The Society of Christian Endeavor grew up as a

necessity for training young converts, and has proved highly beneficial."

Society at Clay Centre, Neb., reports by pastor, Rev. Geo. E.
Taylor: "Society grew out of a revival in January and February."

Society at Belville, N. J., reports through their pastor, Rev. R. W.
Brokaw: "The Society has far more than held its own during the
year. It maintains its Prayer Meetings regularly, and besides has
raised considerable money for church purposes. We consider the
Young People's Society of Christian Endeavor a helpful factor in
our church organization. It develops its members and fits them for
future usefulness in wider spheres. We think that a definite object
for the raising of money is beneficial to the stability of the organization. The Society here is doing a good work, and it could hardly
be spared now from the agencies we employ for the spread of the
truth."

Society at South Natick, Mass., reports by the pastor, Rev. W. D.
P. Bliss: "Ours is a small Congregational Home Mission church,
which a year ago had not forty resident members. Last autumn we
wanted to start a young people's Prayer Meeting, but gave up the idea
because we could get very few young people to come. We went to
work in other ways and God blessed us with a revival. We soon
found young people enough to come, and in March we started a
Young People's Society of Christian Endeavor, and to-day we have
fifty members, forty-two of whom are active. Our Prayer Meetings
are better attended than the church meetings and our monthly consecration meetings are the best we have. * * * We have had
thirty additions to our little church during the year; our Sunday
School has grown; our contributions have grown; but we think
our Young People's Society of Christian Endeavor has done more
and is doing more for our church than anything else. This is simply
to show what the Society has done in a small, old Massachusetts
Home Mission church."

Society at Palmyra, N. Y., reports: "The Society has been doing
a good work in distributing religious reading among the poor of the
church. The interest in the Society work and meetings is growing."

Society at Penn Yan, N. Y., reports through its pastor, Rev. Dr.
Palmer: "This Society was organized only about three months
ago. We call it on the whole a success. We still find it difficult to
work in our young men, and the presence of a number of boys and
girls as members seems to keep away and discourage the very class

of people whom we most desire to reach. The lack of conscience upon the whole matter of social worship and Christian work is the almost insuperable obstacle with us." This and one other are the only reports in which there is any tone of discouragement. Perserverence, faith and earnest work, will with the blessings of God, work wonders.

Society at Poughkeepsie, N. Y., reports by pastor, Rev. Howard B. Grose : " Large increase in membership through a gracious revival which brought 125 new members into the church, 35 of them young men. and all in the Society as active members."

Society at Weedsport, N. Y., reports, " We have had about twelve conversions in the meetings during the winter, eight of the new converts have united with our church and the rest sought homes elsewhere. More are under conviction, and we hope to bring them into the fold."

Society at Providence R. I., reports : " It was thought to be a doubtful experiment in such a church as ours, but now the most skeptical are convinced that it will be a glorious success."

Society at Bethel, Vt., reports : " Society organized with about eleven members and under rather unfavorable circumstances, but by the Grace of God it has prospered. * * * We have gained a recognition in the community which is worth everything, and now, through our help and by our sugggestion, a free reading room is being started with unusually bright prospects."

At the Conference last year it was stated that a Society had been started in Foochow, China. A report has recently been received from it. A brief of its formation has been received of which the following is a copy : " Three years ago or more, Rev. J. E. Walker, missionary of the American Board from China, spoke one Sunday evening in Williston Church, of his ten year's work among the Chinese, and for the first time heard of the S. C. E., and its work among the young people of Williston. On his return to Foochow he found that something was necessary to rouse the Chinese to action, they having the idea that after joining the church nothing more was required of them ; and remembering what he had heard about the help the American young people had, he and his co-workers decided that something of this kind was just what they needed in their work. Accordingly he wrote for full particulars as to the formation of such a society, its methods, &c., which were immediately sent to him, and a letter from him last month states : " Foochow, China, has a S. C.

E., called the 'Ku-la-huoi,' or ' Rouse Up Society,' organized in connection with the work in the suburban station. It has been in operation nearly two months, and is working nicely."

Mr. G. H. Hubbard, a graduate of Yale Seminary (recently associated with Mr. Walker in this field), was familiar with the working of these societies at home, and took the lead in establishing this one. The whole system of organization was quite new to the Chinese christians, and it took some time to organize it; but they now have constitution and by-laws, officers and committees, all complete, and are taking hold with a good deal of enthusiasm. Their meetings are held on Sunday evenings, and at the last one there were about fifty present.

Before closing one thing requires to be presented and pressed upon the notice of the societies, and that is with regard to reports. Out of the 253 societies recorded, 61 have not sent reports this year, and many of them have come in so late that the Secretary has been unable, from lack of time, to present his report in a satisfactory manner. Many details are left out that might be of interest. Let reports in future be certain and very prompt. In closing let us not forget that many of us are in the spring and summer of life, that we have not reached the rich fruitage season of autumn, that if it is to be a rich fruitage season for us there must be the symmetrical, strong, steady, vital growth of the spring and summer of christian endeavor.

Respectfully submitted,

JÁMES W. STEVENSON, *Sec'y.*

Ocean Park, July 8th, 1885.

CALIFORNIA.

Church	City or Town	State	Denomination	When Organized	Active Members	Associate Members	Church Members	United with Ch. since last Conf.	Gain: Active Members	Gain: Associate Members	Loss: Active Members	Loss: Associate Members
First Congregational	Berkley	Cal.	Cong.	February, 1883	40		18	7	10	6		
First Congregational	*Oakland	"	"	Aug. 24, 1882	136		51					
Total					176		69	7	10	6		

CONNECTICUT.

Church	City or Town	State	Denomination	When Organized	Active Members	Associate Members	Church Members	United with Ch. since last Conf.	Gain: Active Members	Gain: Associate Members	Loss: Active Members	Loss: Associate Members
South	Bridgeport	Conn.	Cong.	May 20, 1885	52	1	50					
	Kensington	"	"	Jan. 23, 1883	21	9	19	6				
	Munroe	"	"	February, 1885	18	14	16		7	1		
	New Haven	"	"	April 8, 1884	60	8	34	10				
Second Fair Haven		"	"	Sept., 1884	72	4	66					
Humphrey Street		"	"	April 5, 1883	79	20	49	18			4	2
Howard Avenue		"		Nov. 30, 1884	56		37					
First Congregational	Norwich Town		Pres.	October, 1884	50		60					
First Presbyterian	Thompsonville	"	Cong.	May, 1883	92	25	36	7				
	West Haven	"	"	March 2, 1885	22	29	15					
First Congregational	Winsted	"	Meth.	Sept., 1882	20		43		7			
	*Shelton	"	Cong.	July 1, 1884	43	7		7				
Windsor Avenue	Hartford	"	"	May 8, 1884	61		55		12			
Dwight Place	*New Haven		Meth.	March 1, 1883	64		18	7		25		
	*Birmingham			1881	20		34					
	*Derby	"	Cong.	April 18, 1883	34	44						
	*Easton	"	Baptist	Oct. 1, 1883	40	2	38					
Total					804	172	570	57	26	26	4	2

COLORADO.

Church.	City or Town.	State.	Denomination.	When Organized.	Active Members.	Associate Members.	Church Members.	United with Ch. since last Conf.	Gain Active Members.	Gain Associate Members.	Loss Active Members.	Loss Associate Members.
First Presbyterian	Boulder City	Col.	Pres.	Dec. 11, 1883	20	.	17	15	.	.	11	.
Second Congregational	Denver	"	Cong.	June 1, 1882	43	17	43	.	15	17	.	.
Total					63	17	60	15	15	17	11	.

ILLINOIS.

Church.	City or Town.	State.	Denomination.	When Organized.	Active Members.	Associate Members.	Church Members.	United with Ch. since last Conf.	Gain Active Members.	Gain Associate Members.	Loss Active Members.	Loss Associate Members.
New England	Aurora	Ill.	Cong.	Nov. 1, 1883	60	.	42	15	.	.	.	.
First Congregational	Bunker Hill	"	"	July 27, 1884	30	5	26	.	.	.	.	.
	Geneseo	"	"	Dec., 1884	20	.	20	.	.	.	.	.
First Methodist Episcopal	"	"	Meth.	March, 1884	50	3	40	8	.	.	.	.
Union	Blue Island	"	Cong.	Dec. 7, 1884	23	6	.	.	.	.	.	.
Bethany	Washington Heights	"	Union	May, 1882	27	30	.	.	.	.	.	.
Lutheran	Washington Heights	"	Lutheran		30	3	30	.	.	.	.	.
Total					240	47	158	18	.	.	.	.

BRITISH PROVINCES.

Church.	City or Town.	State.	Denomination.	When Organized.	Active Members.	Associate Members.	Church Members.	United with Ch. since last Conf.	Gain Active Members.	Gain Associate Members.	Loss Active Members.	Loss Associate Members.
St. John	St. John	N. B.	Pres.	June 1, 1885	16	3	16	.	.	.	.	2
Germain Street	"	"	Baptist	Feb. 12, 1883	31	9	31	7	6	.	.	.
Calvary	Montreal	P. Q.	Cong.	October, 1883	40	10	34	8	.	.	.	.
Total					87	22	81	15	6	.	.	2

MAINE.

	Maine	F. Bap	Date								
Court Street		Cong.	Oct. 31, 1883	30	15	35	10	.	.	26	7
Sixth Street		"	Feb., 1884	27	35	96	9	.	.	.	7
High Street		"	Mar. 25, 1882	80	19	67	5	9	4	.	10
Elm Street	Auburn	"	Jan. 20, 1883	30	26	23	.	1	.	.	.
		"	Dec. 1, 1884	34	.	16	7	5	.	.	3
Bucksport		"	Feb. 1, 1883	47	.	38	10	31	8	.	7
Cornish		"	Feb. 8, 1884	93	8	63	30	51	1	.	1
Cumberland Centre		"	April 24, 1885	38	1	.	.	.	.	.	.
Cumberland Mills		Union.	June 6, 1884	32	9	26	5	5	.	3	.
Warren			Feb., 1883	30	4	19	.	.	.	.	.
Second Congregational	Norway	Cong.	Feb. 2, 1881	187	33	142	5	9	8	.	.
Williston	Portland	"	April 26, 1882	57	4	31	9	19	1	.	.
West		"	Feb. 16, 1882	59	33	53	5	7	3	6	.
Second Parish		Baptist	Mar. 2, 1885	33	15	34	.	.	.	.	.
Free Street		Cong.	Dec. 1, 1881	42	30	37	3	2	.	.	.
St. Lawrence Street		F. Bap	Oct. 18, 1882	83	36	76	7	.	.	.	.
Plymouth		Baptist	Feb. 23, 1883	57	21	52	.	.	.	.	.
First Baptist	*	Baptist	Sept. 22, 1884	60	27	50	5	15	1	.	.
Pine Street		Meth.	Sept. 14, 1883	30	10	18	.	.	5	.	.
South Freeport		Cong	April 28, 1883	24	5	12	.	.	.	.	.
West Falmouth		F. Bap.	Dec. 18, 1883	36	4	28	.	.	.	.	.
Buxton		Union	Oct. 20, 1882	65	3	65	.	.	.	.	.
*Woodfords		Cong.	Nov. 10, 1882	23	2	20	.	.	.	.	2
*Kennebunk		"	April 20, 1883	.	.	3	.	.	.	.	.
Union Congregational	Acton		April 20, 1883	7	.	.	.	.	.	.	.
*Paris Hill		Baptist.	Nov. 6, 1883	25	25	21	.	.	.	.	.
First Baptist	Deer Isle	Cong.	Jan. 12, 1884	26	82	11	.	.	.	.	.
First Congregational	Machias		Aug. 1882	29	1	25	.	.	.	.	.
Centre Street	Bluehill	Union.	May 13, 1884	12	34	4	.	.	.	.	.
*Fryeburg		Cong.	Feb. 15, 1884	20	.	15	.	.	.	.	.
First Congregational	Freeport	"	Mar. 3, 1883	36	13	25	.	.	.	.	.
*Bath		"	April 17, 1882	59	.	43	.	.	.	.	.
Limington		"	Dec. 26, 1882	39	3	37	.	.	.	.	.
Total				1424	468	1036	98	154	22	20	39

MASSACHUSETTS.

Church	City or Town	State	Denomination	When Organized	Active Members	Associate Members	Church Members	United with Ch. since last Conf.	Gain Active Members	Gain Associate Members	Loss Active Members	Loss Associate Members
Shawmut	Ashfield	Mass.	Cong.	Jan. 13, '85	46	12	28	4				
Union Congregational	Auburndale	"	"	April '83	61	6	54			1	10	
First Congregational	Boston	"	"	Jan. 19, '85	77	7	77	4				
	Ballardvale	"	"	March, '84	28	11	18					
Harvard	Boxford	"	"	June 7, '85	25	16	16					
First Congregational	Brookline	"	"	April 16, '83	68	74						10
North Avenue	Cambridge	"	"	Oct. 14, '84	120		98	10	20	19		10
First Evan. Congregational	Cambridgeport	"	"	May 20, '83	73	19	68	15	29			9
Winthrop	Charlestown	"	"	Feb. 21, '85	41	10	31	6				
Trinitarian Congregational	Concord	"	"	Oct. 3, '83	73	70	58	10	13	1		
Maple Street	Danvers	"	"	April 24, '83	48	15	44	2	6			
First Congregational	Dedham	"	"	Jan. 1, 85	57	26	49	6				
Second Church	Dorchester	"	"	May 21, '85	28	11	24			11		
	Essex	"	"	April 13, '85	30	32	37	16				
Second Congregational	East Douglas	"	"	Oct. 27, '84	35	32	30				1	
Central	Fall River	"	"	Jan., '84	37	36	36	10				
	Franklin	"	"	Feb. 13, '83	60	48	62	3				
Evan. Congregational	Georgetown	"	"	Mar. 8, '85	33	12	29	1		6		
	Gloucester	"	"	Nov. 4, '84	31	15	31	20				
	Grafton	"	"	Mar. 4, '85	61		43	1	1			
	Granville	"	"	Oct. 22, '82	22	23	22					
First Church	Hadley	"	"		20	10	15					
West	Haverhill	"	"	Mar. 16, '85	41	2	33	25				
North	"	"	"	Jan. 14, '84	34	1	26	2				
	"	"	"	May 2, '82	36				7			

MASSACHUSETTS — Continued.

Church	Town	Denom.	Date										
Second Congregational	Holyoke	Mass.	Oct. 29, '83	37	52	37	12						
First Congregational	Housatonic	Cong.	Feb. 10, '83	19	52	27	11		2				
	Hyde Park	"	Dec. 16, '84	92	18	80	1		3	29			
	Lee	"	April 20, '83	58	30	50	0		3				
	Leicester	Baptist.	April 1, '83	85		16							
Fifth Street	Lowell	Cong.	Nov., '84	56	24	58	1						
Pawtucket		"	Oct. 24, '84	32	10	30	5		25				
High Street		"	Jan. 6, '84	56	65	54	9						
Eliot		"	Oct. 6, '84	61	60	63	2						
John Street		"	Sept. 10, '84	55	37	47	10	28	5				
Kirk Street		"	Mar. 14, '83	90	22	09	6	4	1				
Mount Zion		P. Meth.	Dec., '83	35	7	26							
French Protestant		Cong.	May 6, '85	20	22	15							
Central		"	Dec., '83	52	9	47	9						
North	Lynn	"	Nov. 1, '83	66	20	58	9		10				
Stone Church	Marblehead	"	Sept. 22, '82	50	26	42	5						
	Marion	"	Feb. 21, '85	55	12	13							
	Mattapoisett	"	Mar., '85	22	10	18	1						
Union Congregational	Maynard	"	Mar. 31, '84	37	27	20	5						
Second Congregational	Medfield	"	Sept., '84	29	32	26	1	10	32				
	Melrose	"	Sept. 4, '83	62	42	64		4	10				
First Congregational	Natick	"	1883	55									
	Newton Highlands	"	Mar. 1, '85	34	5	10	1		2				
North	Newburyport	"	Oct., '83	40	31	29	10	6					
North	North Amherst	"	Jan. 14, '85	48	22	36	20						
North Avenue	North Cambridge	Baptist.	Mar. 5, '87	67	12	58							
First Congregational	Rochester	Cong.	Mar., '85	20	7	14	5	13					
	Rockland	"	May 29, '83	45	5	42	16	1	11				
Walnut Avenue	Roxbury	"	Oct. 20, '83	41	46	41	10						
Crombie Street	Salem	"	May '81	24	6	22							
Tabernacle		"	Mar. 9, '85	29	12	28		4					
First Congregational	Shelburne	"	June, '82	22	13	16							
Second Congregational	Shelburne Falls	"	Nov., '84	50	33								3
Broadway	Somerville	"	April 25, '85	25	19	22							

MASSACHUSETTS — Continued.

CHURCH.	Town or City.	State.	Denomination.	When Organized.	Active Members	Associate Members	Church Members	United with Ch. since last Conf.	Gain Active Members	Gain Associate Members	Loss Active Members	Loss Associate Members
Prospect Hill	Somerville	Mass.	Cong.	May 12, '85	33	14	31					
Phillips	South Boston	"	"	Dec. 4, '83	155	65	105	21	17	24		
John Elliot	South Natick	"	"	Feb. 25, '85	41	9	25					
First Church of Christ	Springfield	"	"	April 30, '85	62	7	60	14				12
First Congregational	Sunderland	"	"	Dec. 18, '83	59	15	54		4	9		
First Congregational	Upton	"	"	Feb. 4, '83	49	38	41	32	7	9		
	Walpole	"	"	Jan. '84	29	21	25		3	1		
Union	Wellesley	"	"	Jan. 22, '82	51	30	26	5	2			
	Westford	"	"	Feb. 3, '85	25	0	24					
Second Congregational	West Medford	"	"	Feb. 12, '84	35	17	32	4	9	17		
First Congregational	West Newton	"	"	Oct. 30, '82	38	43	38	2		15	10	
Union	Williamstown	"	"	Mar. 3, '85	31	11	30	1	20			
Old South	Worcester	"	"	Nov. '84	50	3	50					
Piedmont	Worcester	"	"	May 5, '84	41	3	37			3		
Central	Worcester	"	"	Nov. '83	55		53					
Immanuel	*Boston	"	"	Mar. '83	40	10	40					
First Congregational	*Montague	"	"	Feb. 27, '83	59	21	48					
	*Bernardston	"	"	1882	16	20	19					
	*Phillipston	"	"	Nov. 1, '83	12	9	6					
	*Salem	"	"	Apr. 14, '84	19	2	13					
First Baptist	*Salem	"	Baptist.	Mar. '83	60		43					
First Baptist	*Pittsfield	"	"	June 6, '83	40		40					
	*South Egremont	"	Cong.	Mar. 11, '83	21	17	16					
	*Conway	"	"	Nov. 5, '82	35	15	32					
Stoughton Street	*Dorchester	"	"	Oct. '83	48		42					

MASSACHUSETTS — Continued.

Society		State	Denom.	Date							
South	Hatfield	Mass.	Cong.	Oct. 1, '84	21	11					
	South Framingham	"		Dec. 4, '83	38	1	35	8			
	Duxbury	"		Apr. 6, '83	18	44					
	Whitinsville	"		Mar. 7, '84	71						
Day Street Congregational	West Somerville	"			87	24	35				
Total					3973	1706	3107	360	203	227	56	47

IOWA.

Society		State	Denom.	Date						
First Congregational	Cedar Rapids	Iowa	Cong.	Nov., 1884	31	10	29	8	
	Cincinnati	"	"	June, 1885	10	10	10		
	Monticello	"	"	March 25, 1883	36	44	37	5	6	4
First Congregational	Newton	"	"	Dec. 14, 1884	38	30	46	13	
	Pattersonville	"	Union	Oct. 20, 1884	30	29	29	5	
	Rockford	"	Cong.	1884	70	30	13	4	18	5
	Tabor	"	"	May 27, 1884	30	19	30		
	Winthrop	"	"	March 1, 1885	15	15	14		
	Waterloo	"	"	May 14, 1882	50		31		
Total					310	167	229	35	24	9

KANSAS.

Society		State	Denom.	Date				
First Baptist	El Dorado	Kan.	Baptist	October, 1884	40		25	6

MINNESOTA.

Society		State	Denom.	Date					
Pilgrim	Duluth	Minn.	Cong.	Jan. 21, '85	57	10	34	7	
	Glyndon	"	"	Oct. 8, '84	20	12	12		11
Second Congregational	Minneapolis	"	"	Feb., '85	40	15	40	28	
First Congregational	Morris	"	"	Apr. 28, '85	26	1	30		
Total					143	38	106	35	11

MICHIGAN.

Church.	City or Town.	State.	Denomination.	When Organized.	Active Members.	Associate Members.	Church Members.	United with Ch. since last Conf.	Gain Active Members.	Gain Associate Members.	Loss Active Members.	Loss Associate Members.
First Congregational	East Saginaw	Mich.	Cong.	Jan, '85	27	23	20	.	14	.	.	2
First Free Will Baptist	Jackson	"	F. Bap.	Jan, '84	40	3	36	12	.	22	.	.
	Litchfield	"	Union.	Apr. 29, '83	40	34	30	.	5	19	.	.
	St. Joseph	"	Cong.	March, '84	43	21	34	21	18	.	.	.
First Congregational	*Detroit	"	"	Dec. 11, '83	46	10	46	.	.	.	.	.
First Congregational	*Clinton	"	"	Jan. 29, '84	22	2	11	.	.	.	.	.
	*North Adams	"	"	Dec. '82	27	.	7	.	.	.	.	.
Total					245	93	184	33	37	41	.	2

OHIO.

Church.	City or Town.	State.	Denomination.	When Organized.	Active Members.	Associate Members.	Church Members.	United with Ch. since last Conf.	Gain Active Members.	Gain Associate Members.	Loss Active Members.	Loss Associate Members.
First Congregational	Ashtabula	Ohio.	Cong.	Apr. 25, '85	43	.	35	24	.	.	.	.
	Bristolville	"	"	1885	20	.	.	.	.	.	.	.
	Burton	"	"	Feb. 4, '84	73	111	63	.	.	16	.	2
First Congregational	Medina	"	"	May, '84	40	25	40	5	.	.	.	.
	North Bloomfield	"	"	Apr. 23, '85	21	.	.	.	.	.	.	.
	Ravenna	"	"	Dec. '81	74	10	45	.	18	10	.	.
First Congregational	Springfield	"	Pres.	June 19, '85	21	2	21	10	.	2	.	.
First Presbyterian	Zanesville	"	Cong.	Mar. 13, '84	42	20	42	.	22	.	.	.
	*Wellington	"	"	Apr. 15, '84	25	15	25	.	.	.	.	.
	*Madison	"	"	Mar. 21, '82	47	.	35	.	.	.	.	.
Total					406	183	306	39	40	28	.	2

NEBRASKA.

Society	Location	Denom.	Date						
First Congregational	Clay Center	Neb.	Mar. '85	20	1	19	12		
	Weeping Water	"	Jan. 19, '85	30	5	25			
	York	"	Feb. 17, '85	45	12	43			
Total				**95**	**18**	**87**	**12**		

NEW HAMPSHIRE.

Society	Location	Denom.	Date						
First Congregational	Great Falls	N. H. Cong.	Apr. 3, '83	55	8	49		7	
First Congregational	Nashua	"	Nov. '84	59	29		26		
	Newport	"	June 29, '84	31	12	28	14	9	
	*Newmarket	"	Apr. 1, '83	20	12	16			
	*Milton	"	June 4, '83	23		18			2
Total				**188**	**61**	**111**	**40**	**16**	**2**

NEW JERSEY.

Society	Location	Denom.	Date						
Second Reformed	Belville	N. J. Dut. Ref.	Feb., '83	38	15	31	3	5	9
	Chester	Cong.	Apr. 11, '82	14		11		5	1
	Hackensack	Ref.	Mar. 10, '85	50		25	8		
	*Jamesburg	Pres.	Feb. 11, '83	38	6	38			
Total				**140**	**21**	**105**	**11**	**10**	**10**

RHODE ISLAND.

Society	Location	Denom.	Date						
First S. D. Baptist	Ashaway	R. I. S. D. Bap	Feb., '85	34	6	14			
Union	Providence	Cong.	Jan., '85	58	10	58	17		
Pawcatuck S. D. Baptist	Westerly	S. D. Bap	Nov. '84	33	45	33	12		
	*Scituate	Christian	Nov. 22, '81	22	13	15			
Plymouth	*Providence	Cong.	Oct. 3, '82	38	4				
Pawcatuck Congregational	*Westerly	"	Aug. 19, '84	13	12	13			
Total				**198**	**90**	**133**	**29**		

VERMONT.

Church.	City or Town.	State.	Denomination.	When Organized.	Active Members.	Associate Members.	Church Members.	United with Ch. since last Conf.	Gain Active Members.	Gain Associate Members.	Loss Active Members.	Loss Associate Members.
First Congregational	Bethel	Ver.	Cong.	Feb. 28, '85	11	8	9	3				12
College Street	Burlington	"	"	Mar. 15, '83	43	18	44	2	8	8		
Winooski Avenue	"	"	"	Dec., '81	85	28	66	4	10			
First Congregational	Lyndonville	"	"	Jan., '85	60	20	35	1		3		
North Congregational	North Bennington	"	"	June 17, '84	18	18	16	4	6	3		
South Congregational	St. Johnsbury	"	"	Mar. 22, '83	67		57	10	1			
	*Chester	"	"	Mar., '85	82	2	65	28				
	*Brandon	"	"	Oct. 23, '83	26	8	24					
		"	"	Oct., '82	13	15	12					
Total					405	117	328	52	25	11		12

WISCONSIN.

Church.	City or Town.	State.	Denomination.	When Organized.	Active Members.	Associate Members.	Church Members.	United with Ch. since last Conf.	Gain Active Members.	Gain Associate Members.	Loss Active Members.	Loss Associate Members.
First Congregational	Appleton	Wis.	Cong.	Apr. 16, '83	52	20	45	11		5		
	Boscobel	"	"	Sept., '82	25	5	14	10	1	3		
	Clinton	"	"	Feb. 18, '84	26	5	23				4	
First Congregational	Lake Geneva	"	"	Mar. 18, '83	70	14	41					
	*Beloit	"	"	Oct., '82	51	56	13					
	*Racine	"	"	Nov. 14, '82	77				1			
Total					301	100	136	21	1	8	4	

NEW YORK.

Church	City	State	Denom.	Date								
La Fayette Street	Buffalo	N.Y.	Pres.	May 11, '85	44		37	20				4
First Baptist	Chittenango	"	Bap.	July 8, '82	26	10	28				2	
	Fleming	"	Meth.	Apr. 7, '85	15		13	7	10			10
First Presbyterian	Fredonia	"	Pres.	Mar., '83	50	25	50		7	1		
	Newark	"	"	Apr., '83	64	13	66	2		11		
First Baptist	Olean	"	Bap.	June 23, '85	30			30	51			
	Oneida	"	Pres.	May 6, '84	145	19	100					
	Madison	"	Bap.	Oct. 21, '84	24	2	24				20	5
Western Presbyterian	Palmyra	"	Pres.	May, '82	50		50					
	Penn Yan	"	"	Mar. 3, '85	32	29	41					
Baptist Church of Christ	Poughkeepsie	"	Bap.	Jan. 29, '84	100	48	127	61		16		
Central	Rochester	"	Pres.	Apr. 24, '82	62	97	119	15		13		
North	Rochester	"	Pres.	Mar., '84	44	37	70	23	14	17		
Westminster	"	"	"	Oct. 7, '83	50	20	50		1			
	Smyrna	"	Union	Mar. 31, '84	36							
First Baptist	Syracuse	"	Bap.	Dec. 9, '84	44	19	44	11		4		
	Weedsport	"	"	Feb., '84	38	4	36	8		11		
First Presbyterian	Wolcott	"	Pres.	Jan. 22, '83	82	11	74					
	*Potsdam	"	"	May, '84	42	30	28		8			
	*Newburg	"	D. Ref.	Mar. 12, '84	41	11	30		6			
	*Adams Centre	"	Bap.	Oct. 26, '83	21	11	30					
	*Parshville	"	Meth.	June 15, '84	24	17	35					
	*Cortland	"	"	Sept. 17, '83	30		28					
	*Mahopac Falls	"	"	Jan. 16, '83	30		30					
	*Jamestown	"	Cong.	Feb. 23, '83	34	8	21					
Union	Pomfrit	"	"		34	3	32					
First Presbyterian	Verona	"	Pres.	July 5, '85	50							
Total					1242	414	1148	177	98	73	22	19

INDIANA.

Church	City	State	Denom.	Date								
Cumberland and Presbyterian	Evansville	Ind.	Pres.	Apr., '84	65	8	68	10	25			4

MISSOURI.

CHURCH.	City or Town.	State.	Denomination.	When Organized.	Active Members.	Associate Members.	Church Members.	United with Ch. since last Conf.	Gain — Active Members.	Gain — Associate Members.	Loss — Active Members.	Loss — Associate Members.
Pilgrim	St. Louis	Mo.	Cong.	1884	40	20	30					
	*St. Louis	"	"	Nov. 2, '82	48	14	40					
Clyde	*Kansas City	"	"	Sept. 28, '83	32	23	28					
Olivette	*Kansas City	'	'	Dec. 7, '83	21	21	19					
Total					141	78	117					

MARYLAND.

CHURCH.	City or Town.	State.	Denomination.	When Organized.	Active Members.	Associate Members.	Church Members.	United with Ch. since last Conf.	Gain — Active Members.	Gain — Associate Members.	Loss — Active Members.	Loss — Associate Members.
Emery	*Olney	Md.	Meth.	Apr., '83	30		30					

PENNSYLVANIA.

CHURCH.	City or Town.	State.	Denomination.	When Organized.	Active Members.	Associate Members.	Church Members.	United with Ch. since last Conf.	Gain — Active Members.	Gain — Associate Members.	Loss — Active Members.	Loss — Associate Members.
First Presbyterian	Easton	Penn.	Pres.	Mar. 2, '85	20	79	38					
First Baptist	Hatboro	"	Bap.	Mar. 23, '85	14	1	14					
Gaston	Philadelphia	"	Pres.	Feb., '84	48	8	48					
Butler Street	Pittsburgh	"	Meth.	Mar. 20, '85	126	11	112	63				
	*Scranton		Cong.	July, '82	100	....	90					
Total					308	99	302	63				

WASHINGTON TERRITORY.

CHURCH.	City or Town.	State.	Denomination.	When Organized.	Active Members.	Associate Members.	Church Members.	United with Ch. since last Conf.	Gain — Active Members.	Gain — Associate Members.	Loss — Active Members.	Loss — Associate Members.
First Congregational	*Seattle	W. Ter	Cong.	Mar. 4, '83	32	10	11	3		8	1	
	Tacoma	"	"	Feb., '84	9	15	8	3		8	1	
Total					41	25	19	3		8	1	

* These figures are taken from previous report.

SUMMARY.

States.	Societies.	Active Members.	Associate Members.	Total Members.	Church Members.	United with Church.	Loss.		Gain.		Net Active and Assoc.	
							Active.	Associate.	Active.	Associate.	Loss.	Gain.
California . .	2	176		176	69	7			10	6		16
Connecticut . . .	17	804	172	976	570	57			26			26
Colorado	2	63	17	80	60		11		15	17		21
Illinois	6	210	44	254	128	18						
Indiana	1	65	8	73	68	10			25			25
Iowa	9	310	187	497	229	35			24	9		33
Kansas	1	40		40	25	6						
Maine	32	1,424	468	1,892	1,036	98	29	39	154	22		108
Maryland . . .	1	30		30	30							
Massachusetts .	88	3,936	1,682	5,618	3,072	360	55	47	203	227		328
Michigan	7	245	93	338	184	33		2	37	41		76
Minnesota . . .	4	143	38	181	106	35				11		11
Missouri	4	141	78	219	117							
Nebraska	3	95	18	113	87	12						
New Hampshire .	5	188	61	249	111	40			16	2		18
New Jersey . . .	4	140	21	155	105	11			10	10		20
New York	25	1,258	411	1,569	1,116	177	22	19	98	73		130
Ohio	10	406	183	589	306	39	2		40	28		66
Oregon	1	50		50	25							
Pennsylvania .	5	308	99	407	302	63						
Rhode Island . .	6	198	90	288	133	29						
Vermont	9	405	117	522	328	52		12	25	11		24
Washingt'n Territory	2	41	25	66	19	3	1			8		7
Wisconsin	6	301	100	401	136	21	4		1	8		5
Dominion of Canada	3	87	22	109	81	15		2	6			4
Total	253	10,964	3,934	14,892	8,443	1,121	124	121	690	473		*918

* This is the gain made by the various societies since last conference, and is not to be confounded with the gain by new societies reported for first time this year.

THE MODEL CONSTITUTION.

This constitution has been prepared with great care, and seemed to meet with the very general endorsement of the Fourth Annual Conference at Ocean Park.

It is not intended to be binding upon any local society, but is to be regarded simply in the light of a recommendation, especially for the guidance of new organizations and those unacquainted with the work of the Society of Christian Endeavor. It is hoped, however, for the sake of uniformity, that the *constitution*, which deals only with main principles, may be generally adopted, and that such changes as may be needed to adapt the society to local needs will be made in the By-Laws. The specimen By-Laws which are here appended embrace suggestions for the government of the society, which have been found successful in many places. Each one is approved by experience.

MODEL CONSTITUTION.

ARTICLE I.—NAME.

This Society shall be called THE YOUNG PEOPLE'S SOCIETY OF CHRISTIAN ENDEAVOR.

ARTICLE II.—OBJECT.

Its object shall be to promote an earnest christian life among its members, to increase their mutual acquaintance, and to make them more useful in the service of God.

ARTICLE III.—MEMBERSHIP.

1. The members shall consist of two classes, Active and Associate.

2. Active members. The Active members of this society shall consist of all young persons who believe themselves to be christians, and who sincerely desire to accomplish the results above specified.

3. Associate members. All young persons of worthy character, who are not at present willing to be considered decided Christians, may become Associate members of this society. They shall have the special prayers and sympathy of the Active members, but shall be excused from taking part in the prayer meeting. It is expected that all Associate members will regularly attend the prayer meetings, and that they will in time become Active members, and the society will work to this end.

4. They shall become members upon being elected by the society, after carefully examining the constitution, and upon signing their names to it, thereby pledging themselves to live up to its requirements.

ARTICLE IV.—OFFICERS.

1 The officers of this society shall be a President, Vice President, Secretary and Treasurer, who shall be chosen from among the Active members.

2. There shall also be a Lookout Committee, a Prayer meeting Committee, a Social Committee, and such other committees as the local needs of each society may require, each consisting of five Active members.

ARTICLE V.—DUTIES OF OFFICERS.

1. President; The President of the society shall perform the duties usually pertaining to that office. He shall have especial watch over the interests of the society, and it shall be his care to see that the different committees perform the duties devolving upon them.

2 Vice President; The Vice President shall perform the duties of the President in his absence.

3. Secretary; It shall be the duty of the Secretary to keep a record of the members. and to correct it from time to time, as may be necessary, and to obtain the signature of each newly elected member to the constitution: also to correspond with absent members, and inform them of their standing in the society; also to keep correct minutes of all business meetings of the society; also to notify all persons elected to office or to committees, and to do so in writing, if necessary.

4. Treasurer; It shall be the duty of the Treasurer to safely keep all monies belonging to the society, and to pay out only such sums as shall be voted by the society.

ARTICLE VI.—DUTIES OF COMMITTEES.

1 Lookout Committee: It shall be the duty of this Committee to bring new members into the society, to introduce them to the work and to the other members, and to affectionately look after and reclaim any that seem indifferent to their duties. This committee shall also, by personal investigation, satisfy themselves of the fitness of young persons to become members of this society, and shall propose their names at least one week before their election to membership.

2. Prayer meeting Committee: This Committee shall have in charge the prayer meeting, shall see that a topic is assigned and a leader appointed for each meeting, and shall do what it can to secure faithfullness to the prayer meeting pledge.

3. Social Committee: It shall be the duty of this Committee to promote the social interests of the society, by welcoming strangers to the meetings and by providing for the mutual acquaintance of the members by occasional sociables, for which any appropriate entertainment may be provided.

4. Each committee shall make a report in writing to the society at the monthly business meeting, concerning the work of the past month.

ARTICLE VII.—THE PRAYER MEETING.

1 It is expected that all the members shall be present at every meeting, unless detained by some absolute necessity, and that each Active member shall take some part, however slight, in every meeting. The meetings shall be held just one hour, and at the close some time may be taken for introduction, and social intercourse, if desired.

2. Once each month an Experience or Consecration Meeting shall be held, at which each Active Member shall speak concerning his progress in the Christian life. If anyone chooses, he can express his feelings by an appropriate verse of Scripture or other quotation.

3. At each Experience or Consecration Meeting, the roll shall be called, and the response of the Active Members who are present shall be considered as a renewed ex-

pression of allegiance to Christ. It is expected that if anyone is obliged to be absent from this meeting, he will send the reason for such absence by someone who attends.

4. If any Active Member of this society is absent from this monthly meeting and fails to send an excuse, the Lookout Committee is expected to take the name of such a one, and, in a kind and brotherly spirit, ascertain the reason for the absence. If any Active Member of the society is absent and unexcused from three consecutive monthly meetings, such a one ceases to be a member of the society, and his name shall be stricken from the list of members.

ARTICLE VIII.—Business Meetings and Elections.

1 Business Meetings may be held at the close of the evening prayer-meeting, or at any other time in accordance with the call of the President.

2. An Election of Officers and Committees shall be held once in six months. Names may be proposed by a Nominating Committee appointed by the President.

ARTICLE IX.—Relation to the Church.

This Society being in closest relation to the Church, the Pastor, Deacons, Elders or Stewards, and Sunday School Superintendent shall be ex-officiis, Honorary Members. Any difficult question may be laid before them for advice.

ARTICLE X.—Withdrawals.

Any Member who may wish to withdraw from the society shall state the reasons in writing to the Lookout Committee and Pastor, and if these reasons seem sufficient, they may, by a *two-thirds vote of the society*, be allowed to withdraw.

ARTICLE XI.—Miscellaneous.

1. Any other Committees may be added and duties assumed by this society which in the future may seem best.

2 This Constitution may be amended by a two-thirds vote of the members present, provided that notice of such Amendment be given in writing, and recorded by the Secretary, at least one week before the Amendment is acted upon.

By-Laws.
ARTICLE I.

This Society shall hold a Prayer Meeting on————evening of each week. The last regular Prayer Meeting of each month shall be an Experience or Consecration Meeting, at which the roll shall be called.

ARTICLE II.
OPTIONAL METHOD OF CONDUCTING THE EXPERIENCE OR CONSECRATION MEETING.

At this meeting the roll may be called by the leader during the meeting, instead of at its close. After the opening exercises, the names of five or more may be called, and then a hymn sung or prayer offered. Thus varied, with singing and prayer interspersed, the entire roll may be called.

ARTICLE III.

This Society shall hold its regular Business Meeting, for members only, at the close of the first regular prayer-meeting in the month. Special Business Meetings at the call of the President. At all business meetings, the Associate Members shall be privileged to take part in the discussion, but shall not be allowed to vote on the question.

ARTICLE IV.

Other committees may be added according to the needs of local societies, whose duties may be defined as follows:

THE SUNDAY SCHOOL COMMITTEE.

It shall be the duty of this Committee to endeavor to bring into our Sunday School those who do not attend elsewhere, and to co-operate with the Superintendent and officers of the school, in any ways which they may suggest for the benefit of the Sunday School.

THE CALLING COMMITTEE.

It shall be the duty of this Committee to have a special care for those among the young people who do not feel at home in our midst, to call on them, and to remind others where calls should be made.

MUSIC COMMITTEE.

It shall be the duty of this Committee to provide for the singing at the Tuesday evening meeting, and also to turn the musical ability of the Society to account, when necessary, at public religious meetings.

MISSIONARY COMMITTEE.

It shall be the duty of this Committee to provide for an occasional missionary meeting, to interest the members of the Society in all ways in missionary topics, and to aid in any manner which may seem practicable, the cause of home and foreign missions.

FLOWER COMMITTEE.

It shall be the duty of this Committee to provide flowers for the pulpit and to distribute them to the sick at the close of the Sabbath services. *

TEMPERANCE COMMITTEE.

It shall be the duty of this Committee to do what may be deemed best to promote temperance principles and sentiment among the members of the Society.

If it is thought that these rules and regulations are unnecessarily long, it should be borne distinctly in mind that these specimen By-Laws are simply *suggestions*. It is not recommended that they be adopted entire, as in the case of the Model Constitution, for all of them would not be adapted, perhaps, to the need of any one society, but from them all valuable *hints* may be derived for the government of local organizations. The fundamental principles of the Society are exceedingly simple (as explained elsewhere), and only so many of the above rules need be adopted as seem necessary to the easy working of this plan for Christian nurture   Undue attention to rules and parliamentary law is to be deprecated, and the fundamental fact that the object of this Society *is solely for Christian work and growth* should never be lost out of sight.

ARTICLE V.

The election of Officers and Committees shall be held at the first business meeting in ————and————. A Nominating Committee shall be appointed by the President, of which the pastor may be a member, ex-officio.

While membership on the board of officers or committees of this society should be distributed as evenly as the best good of the Society will warrant among the different members, the offices should not be considered places of honor to be striven for, but simply opportunities for increased usefulness, and any ill feeling or jealousy springing from this cause shall be deemed unworthy a member of the Society of Christian En deavor. When, however, a member has been fairly elected, it is expected that he will consider his office a sacred trust, to be conscientiously accepted, and never to be declined except for most urgent and valid reasons. The above clause of the By-Laws may be read before each semi-annual election of officers.

ARTICLE VI.

All applications for membership shall be made on printed forms which shall be supplied by the Lookout Committee, and returned to them for consideration. Names may be proposed for membership at the close of the Experience Meetings, and shall be voted on by the Society at the following Business Meeting. The Lookout Committee may also, in order to satisfy itself of the Christian character of the candidate, present to all candidates for Active Membership the following card to be signed:

Trusting in the Lord Jesus Christ for strength, I promise Him that I will try to do whatever He would like to have me do; that I will pray to Him and read the Bible every day, and that, just so far as I know how, *throughout my whole life I will try to lead a Christian life.*

                    Signed ....

ARTICLE VII.

Persons who have forfeited their membership may be readmitted on recommendation of the Lookout Committee and the pastor, and a two-thirds vote of the members present at any regular business meeting.

ARTICLE VIII.

New members shall sign the Constitution and By-Laws within two weeks from their election, to confirm the vote of the Society.

ARTICLE IX.

Any who cannot accept the office to which they may be elected shall notify the President in writing before the next Business Meeting, at which the vacancy shall be filled.

ARTICLE X.

Membership tickets may be furnished to all members of the Society, admitting them to all the Sociables. The Social Committee may furnish tickets to members for their friends, providing they are suitable persons, admitting them to the Sociable dated on the ticket.

ARTICLE XI.

The Lookout Committee shall read the names of any who may cease to be members, and give the reason why their names should be taken off the list.

ARTICLE XII.

Cards of Dismission to other Christian Endeavor Societies shall be given to members *in good standing* who apply in writing to be released from their obligations to the Society. This release to take effect when they shall become members of another Society; until then, their names shall be kept on the Absent List. Members removing to other places, or desiring to join other Christian Endeavor Societies in this city, are requested to obtain Cards of Dismission and Recommendation within six months from the time of their leaving us, unless they shall give satisfactory reasons to the Society for their further delay. These Cards shall be good for six months only.

ARTICLE XIII.

Members who cannot meet with us for a time are requested to obtain a Leave of Absence, which shall be granted by the Society on recommendation of the Lookout Committee and pastor, and their names shall be placed on the Absent List.

ARTICLE XIV.

———————— members shall constitute a quorum.

ARTICLE XV.

These By-Laws may be amended by a two-thirds vote of the members present.

THE YOUNG PEOPLE'S SOCIETY OF CHRISTIAN ENDEAVOR. — WHAT IT IS. HOW IT WORKS, AND HOW TO FORM A SOCIETY.

BY REV. F. E. CLARK, BOSTON.

The Young People's Society of Christian Endeavor is simply an *organised effort* to lead the young people to Christ and into His church, to establish them firmly in the faith, and to set them at work in the Lord's vineyard. The main point upon which the constitution insists is the weekly prayer-meeting, which *each active member pledges himself or herself to attend* (unless detained by some absolute necessity) *and to participate in, in some way,* if only by a repetition of a verse of Scripture.

Once each month a special meeting of reconsecration to Christ is held, at which special pains are taken to see whether every active member is faithful to his pledge and true to Christ. The society may, and, as an actual fact, often does, branch off into many other departments of Christian effort, adapting itself to the local needs of each church, *but these rules concerning the prayer-meeting are imperative; without them there cannot be a true Society of Christian Endeavor.*

A society thus organized among the young people has proved itself to be in many cases

A HALF-WAY HOUSE TO THE CHURCH.

Into this society the new Christian, however young or feeble he may be, may come at once. Here he may at once be recognized as a Christian, may at once have the opportunity and be encouraged to acknowledge his Saviour, and at once be set to work for Him. To use another figure, this society bridges the dangerous gap between conversion and church membership, which is often a long one in the case of young disciples, an interval when many stray away, and are lost forever to the church and the Christian cause.

This society is also

A TRAINING SCHOOL IN THE CHURCH.

It gives the young Christian something to do at once.

It accustoms him to the sound of his own voice in the prayer meeting.

It causes him to understand that he has a part to perform in the activities of the church, as well as the oldest Christian. It sends him upon a hundred errands for Christ. Very soon he learns that he has a duty in the general church prayer-meetings, and he becomes naturally and easily one of the pastor's trusted helpers.

This society is also a

WATCH-TOWER FOR THE CHURCH.

The pastor ought always to attend the prayer-meetings and the social gatherings, and, unseen, keep his hands on the reigns of the organization. If he does so, wisely and constantly, he cannot help knowing how the young converts are progressing in the Christian life.

No month need ever go by without the pastor knowing the religious status of each of his young people.

THE COMMITTEES.

The various committees are very important features of the Young People's Society of Christian Endeavor. With faithful, earnest, intelligent committees, the work can hardly fail to succeed. Perhaps the most important committee is the "Lookout Committee." This committee has for part of its work to introduce new members to the society, and *it needs to take great pains that only those who have begun the Christian life are thus introduced as active members.* But its most delicate, and at the same time important duty, is the reclaiming of those who have grown lax and indifferent to their vows. The very fact that this committee is on the "lookout" will prove a salutary restraint upon many. There are few young people who stay away who cannot be reclaimed and brought back to their allegiance by a wise and faithful Lookout Committee.

The other committees, especially the Prayer Meeting and Social Committees, are scarcely less important, but their duties are easily understood, as defined in the constitution, and we do not need to dwell upon their work.

All these committees, according to their zeal and devotion, can make much or little of their office. Each one of them affords a grand opportunity for efficient service, if it is rightly used.

WHO MAY BECOME MEMBERS?

Should there be an age limit? These are questions which are often asked. We are not in favor of a strict age limit, since youth and age are such variable terms. Many a man is old at twenty-five. Many a man is fifty is still young. This matter can usually be left to the sanctified common sense of Christian men and women. It is very essential that there should be in the society a number of the older young people, say, those between twenty and thirty-five, to give stability to the work and to take the lead in the committees. On the other side the age limit easily takes care of itself. Children whom their parents allow to be out in the evening are not too young to become members.

THE EXPERIENCE MEETING.

This meeting is one of great importance. It may be called by various names: "Experience," "Consecration," "Progress," or simply the "Monthly Meeting," but by whatever name it is called, it should and may be made a real power. *At this meeting, in some way some expression of renewed loyalty to Christ should be obtained from every active member.* When the roll is called it should be made a very serious matter, and the mere response to the name should be considered a reconsecration. Some societies have found it best to call the roll, not at the close, but during the progress of the meeting, so that each may respond to his name with a prayer, or a word of testimony, or a passage of Scripture. This plan for many societies is the best.

THE ASSOCIATE MEMBERS.

The duties of the Active Members are plain enough: humble Christian living, constant attendance upon the meetings, and constant participation. The duties of the Associate Members are less easily defined. They are the young people who, while they are not willing to avow themselves active Christians, are willing to put themselves under Christian influences, and are willing to receive the prayers of the Active Members. That they owe something to the society is plain. In many societies attendance upon the meetings is required from the Associate Members, but not participation in the meetings. At the Experience Meeting in some societies their names are called, for the purpose of finding out if they are present, not for the purpose of obtaining a renewed consecration. Every good influence should be kept around such members, and every effort made to bring them to Christ.

HOW TO FORM A SOCIETY.

Begin with as many earnest, active young Christians as are available for this work. Do not be anxious for numbers. Think more of quality than quantity. Half a score of those who are earnest and consecrated are worth in this work ten score of half-hearted ones. A *very few* young people of the right sort can make a strong Society of Christian Endeavor. If the Society begins right, it is sure to grow. *Do not lower the standard or cater to the worldly laxness of the average Christian by making the way in easy.* The great danger is just in this line—that many will rush in at first who have no proper conception of their obligations, and who will prove a positive source of weakness to the Society. *Make sure that everyone who joins fully understands his duties and obligations, and is willing, in Christ's strength, to undertake them.* Call together the earnest young Christians who are thus willing to pledge themselves to this work, let them adopt and sign the constitution, which act solemnly pledges them to a performance of these duties, let them choose their officers and committees, and the Society is formed and ready to go forward with its work.

SUMMARY.

The essential features, then, of the Young People's Society of Christian Endeavor are pledged and constant attendance upon the weekly prayer-meetings, pledged and *constant participation therein by every active member,* pledged and constant work for others, through the committees and in any way which may be suggested. A few, living up to these pledges faithfully, will, with the blessing of God, soon become a powerful host in any church. *There is no danger that the rules will be too strictly enforced. There is great danger that they will be regarded too loosely. The society that looks to God for all blessings and strictly observes their vows, voluntarily taken by each young person, cannot fail.* More can be learned concerning the society from a careful study of the constitution than in any other way, perhaps. Hundreds of different constitutions have been printed, differing in minor, local matters, in the number of committees, etc., but all which represent true Societies of Christian Endeavor agree in the fundamental rules which relate to the prayer-meeting and pledged consecration to Christian service.

PRESIDENT'S ADDRESS.

MR. W. H. PENNELL, PORTLAND, MAINE.

REVIEW OF THE YEAR.

For the fourth time the Young People's Society of Christian Endeavor meets in General Conference. Few are its years thus far, but wonderful has been its progress. Beginning with one branch of Christ's Church, it has worked its way into hundreds of others. Brought into life amid the ice and snow of a northern winter, it has gone, not like the ice and snow, to chill, but with the power of the Sun of Righteousness to warm and vivify the souls of the children of men. Like the snow that covers all with a mantle of purity, hiding all landmarks and boundaries, so it is our endeavor to hide all denominational differences under the mantle of Christian fellowship. And so we meet here under the pines and by the sounding sea to look at our work, not along a narrow line of denominational distinction, but over the broad field as Christians. A broad field indeed is ours already, not confined to this country or to this continent, but like that field spoken of by the Master, it is "white already to harvest, but the laborers are few." Let it be our endeavor while here to devise ways and means "to send forth laborers into this harvest."

Our Annual Conferences have been the means, under God, of carrying the work far and wide; by the interest developed, and by the printed reports furnished to all that we could reach, the Society has become a household word in thousands of homes. This year over which we look in review has been a year of rapid progress in the growth and influence of our Society. This is more evident, perhaps, in the kindly, earnest way in which the religious papers recommend the work to their readers, and in the great desire expressed by pastors who have been blessed with a revival, that a Society of Christian Endeavor might be established in their churches, to train their converts in christian knowledge, and to make them more useful in the service of God. It is no longer thought to be sufficient to catch the penitent and land him in the church to die of spiritual inanition and homesickness perhaps, but rather to enlist him as a soldier of Christ's army, and then to train him for the warfare, fitting upon him the whole armor of God; teaching him to use it especially in winning other souls to Jesus, his captain. And here is the strong side of our organization, a training school for our churches; not a West Point simply where only a few may be fitted to be leaders, but where each may learn how best to use the talents God has given.

A glance at a small per centage of the letters received the past year would convince any one that the church universal is ready for this work, and that the expenditure of the few dollars—reaching but a little way into the hundreds—during the past four years, has been the means of doing more good than hundreds of times as much in any one denominational line of christian work. We claim a home and warm welcome in every evangelical church, and all are our friends, if they love and serve the Lord Jesus Christ; and the Society of Christian Endeavor cannot in any way ever antagonize the church, for we are in the church, of the church, and for the church.

The expenditure for the four years, from the general fund, has been $300. This does not include, of course, what has been spent by individuals in postage and traveling expenses, nor what has been expended by our Treasurer from his private purse in sending publications far and wide. No one can cry out yet over wasted contributions and great executive expense. The Treasurer's Report will give in detail the receipts and expenditures, and to that I invite your attention.

It has been demonstrated that the Young Peoples' Society of Christian Endeavor is worthy to take its place with other plans for the evangelization of the world, and this can only be done by united effort. We have no right to assume that some one will do the work and pay all the bills and push the work to its completion, which is the salvation of the last child on earth. We have come up to the entrance into the promised land, the door is open, the command is, "go up and possess the land." Shall we do it? It depends upon you to decide this question during this conference. It was voted at the last conference that the Executive Committee secure an act of incorporation for the better carrying out of the work. After weighing the whole matter very carefully for some months, it was thought best to avail ourselves of the general law of the State of Maine, and so, under this, the incorporation has been completed.

It is expected that a regular income will be secured for the work of the society by the aid of membership fees or life membership certificates, or still more by liberal bequests from our wealthy friends. This does not imply that we wish our friends to die in order that we may become rich; we want them to see the returns from their investments for many years. Nor does it imply that each society and individual will be free from all responsibility in the matter; it will rather increase our opportunities to use our contributions in making members or life members of our favorite workers.

At the conference in Lowell last year, it was thought best to recommend that each member of the various societies be requested to contribute ten cents for the use of the General Conference. A circular was prepared and sent out, stating for what purpose the money was to be used. The returns were not what we hoped, and so our financial matters have been rather limited, delaying the work somewhat and preventing the Executive Committee from carrying out what they desired in spreading the work. It seems to me we should encourage very strongly the missionary spirit in our societies, and endeavor to train each one in systematic giving. Some have adopted monthly contributions at the Experience Meeting, others set the amount at so much per month, and expect their members to be as faithful to their financial pledge as to that of the Prayer Meeting.

We have felt very seriously the past year the need of some way by which all societies could be reached; a need that can only be answered, it seems to me, by a *society paper*, by means of which information can be sent out. In many cases we have known only the name of the pastor of the church where societies exist. When, for any reason, the pastor has left, our communications fail to reach the society, and of course they will feel that they are slighted or ignored. We think that even in our smallest societies one or more copies of a society paper would be taken, and so the bond of union would be maintained. I would respectfully request your thoughtful attention to the discussion of this subject during this conference.

Our Executive Committee, feeling the need of some way in which the constantly recurring question, " What is the Society of Christian Endeavor?" might be answered readily and surely, requested Rev. Mr. Clark, the founder of the society, to prepare a small tract giving concisely all that was required to be known. This was done promptly, and several thousand copies have been printed, and they have been sent far and wide. The conference reports of last year have been sent to all who have favored us with their address. Of this report 2,000 copies were printed; a very few only remain in hand. The preparation of the matter for the printer and the entire oversight of this most important work was undertaken gratuitously by Rev. S. W. Adriance, of Lowell. The work was performed under great difficulties, but was completed with the utmost speed possible under the circumstances. Our gratitude is due to Mr. Adriance for the faithful manner in which he carried out the request of your Executive Committee, and I trust some acknowledgment of this service will be made during the conference. The last conference directed that blanks should be prepared for semi-yearly reports. This has not been done, although the necessity of such was made very apparent. The delay has been simply for want of funds. We desire that all should know the extent and spread of the work for mutual encouragement. To this end we desire to know where societies are located and with whom we may communicate. As this is for the interest of all, will not all interest themselves to assist the Executive Committee?

The same need exists in each society of knowing where their members are. As the years go on, the absent lists will grow larger. What shall we do about it? Is a member no longer a member because he is a few miles away; though still engaged in Christian endeavor? Is it not the duty of each society to keep the connection good by correspondence? It is the rule of one society that absent members shall report in three or six months, or be dropped from the rolls for neglecting to do so. Tender and fraternal letters have been the result of this plan, coming sometimes thousands of miles, containing assurances of their faithfulness. I would suggest that some attention be given to this matter by the conference, and if thought best, some plan be recommended for adoption. And in this connection I would mention the plan of certificates of membership, a plan adopted by the society in Foochow. China, of which you will hear more during the meeting of the conference.

During the past year it has been more than ever difficult to reply by personal letters to all the kind friends who have favored us with communications; we have tried to forward promptly all reports and circulars asked for. Should any feel slighted because such have not reached them, we hope they will not condemn us for lack of interest. Some applications have reached us containing simply the name upon a postal card, without town or state, leaving us to guess where they live, if the mailing stamp proves illegible.

In closing, let me urge upon all a more thorough plan of fellowship meetings among societies. I think they should be encouraged to the fullest extent, and frequent county gatherings, and certainly once each year a state convention, would be found almost indispensable to those who desire the fullest returns for their endeavors. Our work is so widespread that we cannot meet in any place that is not a great way off for many of our members, and yet the inspiration of these meetings is so strong and helpful that the more they can be enjoyed, the sooner will our work be accomplished.

If this conference should authorize the Executive Committee to employ a General Secretary who shall be able to give his whole time to this work, the most pleasing labor he will have to do will be to attend these state conventions and encourage the hearts of the friends by his acquaintance with the work as a whole. This subject will be presented to you by Rev. F. E. Clark, and to that I invite your prayerful attention. This matter must be attended to by ourselves, for we have no one denomination to go to and request help. Let us look the matter bravely in the face and settle it as for God. And now I have the honor to leave these matters with you, knowing that you will weigh them well, and if there is merit in any suggestion, your endeavor will be to look at them as Christians, and to so decide them that " He

> From out whose hand
> The centuries fall like grains of sand

will, in the ages to come, show us the exceeding riches of His grace in kindness towards us in Christ Jesus."

ASSOCIATE MEMBERS.

BY REV. S. WINCHESTER ADRIANCE, LOWELL, MASS.

I have been asked to open up a subject in which I would rather be a pupil than a teacher. I notice that in the two conferences preceding this there has been no paper on "The Associate Membership." At each of those conferences many questions have been propounded and differently answered. There is a wide difference in the various methods in which this branch is used. You cannot hope that I shall bring to you any satisfying solution to the question, "What use shall we make of the Associate Membership?"

1. As to the idea of this branch. The active branch has to do with those who are Christians. The associate must therefore deal with those who are not. The original constitution expressly, and it seems to me wisely, asserts this. As it is the idea of the active membership to develop the power of the young Christian, it must be the idea of the associate membership to touch and win those who are not Christians. If one who is a Christian is a member of this associate branch, it must be from one of three reasons. We may imagine, first, some who are really Christians, and yet have never dared to call themselves such. There are, secondly, those who can only come occasionally, and so join this branch, since the active members are required to be present at each meeting. There are, third, those who want the blessings of the society, but none of its responsibilities. They are disinclined to take part because it is hard. Now the question comes, is it wise for the society to receive these into the associate membership? The difficulty of the question relates to the two latter classes, those who can come occasionally, but are willing then to do all they can, and those who are unwilling to make the effort which the active member's pledge suggests. As to the former, I wish we might make some arrangement other than putting them into the associate membership. Indeed, in some societies there is the same requirement of attendance on the associates as on the actives.

But ought those who are unwilling to make the effort and sacrifice required in taking part in these meetings be welcomed to the associate membership? Will it not, instead of spurring the weak ones to greater endeavors, provide for them what they have had in the church meetings heretofore, viz., a comfortable seat where they can listen and be helped. As I take it, the object of this whole movement is to rouse every Christian to endeavors. He is told that our duty is not to be ministered to, but to minister. It is this valiant struggle to overcome diffidence and all other difficulties to which the active membership has called which has brought about the success of the movement.

The precedent which is created in any one society, when a Christian goes into the associate branch, is very dangerous. Some have avoided this, or tried to, by increasing the responsibilities of the Associate Members. They are required to be present; are asked to send excuses when absent.

The fact is, that while there is great uniformity in the idea of the Active Membership, there is a distracting variation in the idea and method of the Associate Members. The original constitution, which most of the societies have adopted literally, is somewhat vague. One realizes that the heart of the founder was absorbed in the great desire to develope the younger Christians.

In accordance with the opinion set forth above, which may be taken for what it is worth, the Associate Membership, in the founder's mind, was meant to be the intermediate step between the world and the Christian life, and not the backward step from the active Christian life, and the world-life. It seems to me, therefore, that the associate branch represents the work of this society in touching and winning the unsaved young. There are thus the two great Endeavors, the first of which, so gloriously successful, to make all young Christians, down to the very weakest, active in service, the second, the work of saving the others. How, then, is the Associate Membership to be so constituted as to bring the young to the Lord Jesus Christ? •

(*a*) Endeavor to keep the Christians out of it. It is as necessary to get all who are Christians into an active relation to the society. It does not occur that we ought to encourage invalidism. The having the names of Christians on the associate roll, the becoming accustomed to the thought that many such can come night after night and yet not contribute to the meeting, will hinder the non-Christian. It will do much to make worthless that sentence of the constitution: "It is hoped and expected that all associate members will in time become active members." If we are to complete the work among the unsaved, we want to keep the thought before them, that it is expected of them, as soon as they become Christians, that they seek to be active for the Lord. How is this thought sustained if facts show them that it is not expected?

(*b*) But another wrong is done to the unsaved if those who should be active are only associate. They cannot honestly unless the constitution is altered. It provides that "any person who is not willing to be considered a decided Christian may be an Associate Member." How, then, can an active member unite with this branch without deliberately making a negative confession that he is not willing to be considered a decided Christian? And will not this tend to give an impression wholly injurious to those not Christians on this branch?

(*c*) That the Associate Membership may be effective in throwing around its members a healthy Christian influence, it must be as constant as possible. To be constant implies the assuming on the part of Associate Members some pledge of attendance. In many of our societies this is the case, and a most wise provision it seems to me. The Associate Membership ought to be counted worth something. If there are no requisites and its members can come and go as they please, it is valued accordingly. We believe this has been the fault of this branch. Still, there must be a caution. There must be found that blessed mean where there is sufficient requirement to make it an honorable and helpful matter, and yet not so much as to keep the young away. It will not do for us to tighten the wrench too much. Our constitution does not clearly set forth what is to be done. It says: "It is expected that all the active members * * will be present at every meeting." We also favor the calling of the names of the Associate Members at the Experience Meeting, not for an expression of Christian hope, but to find out their presence or absence. And yet at such a meeting, gathering courage from the mere answering of their name, there is the hope that it may furnish the needed occasion for their consecration to the Christian life.

(*d*) There is needed some clearer setting forth, what are the privileges of the Associate Members. Reading our constitution literally, they already have all the privileges save taking part in the meetings. It says: "Such an one shall have all the privileges of the society, and shall have the special prayers and sympathy of the active members, but shall be excused from taking part in the prayer meetings." Several of the later constitutions add this clause: "These officers and committees shall be chosen from among the active members." Yet it seems to me that this is going too far. While it is eminently proper that the members of the prayer-meeting and a majority of the members of the Outlook and Social Committees shall be active members, it may be also the link between the past life and the coming Christian life to give them something to do. The flower committee might be entirely composed of the Associate Members, and they might have a minority representation on some of the other committees. Indeed, the Associate Members may have great influence in inducing other unconverted young people to attend the meetings. It may be a question worth considering whether there shall not be an Outlook Committee of seven, two of whom shall be Associate Members; or, if it be better, an Associate Outlook Committee. We want, however, to avoid too many complications. As the work of the Society broadens, this will be the tendency. What seems plain to us will not seem so to those who are thinking over the matter of forming a society.

SUITABLE AND SUFFICIENT LITERATURE.

BY REV. C. A. STONE, RAVENNA, OHIO.

The question of the hour is, what does this society need to make it not only efficient, but competent to do what seems important to do? It has the most promising field of America. Has it not the material to make the best workers? Who are better able to reach and save the young than the young themselves—if they know how? It is true that we need numbers, organization, rules, committees, system, but system will fail without intelligence. Instruction is needed, teaching, line upon line, precept upon precept, in Biblical lore. We need to-day the laying of solid foundations in knowledge. We have a special field, a special service, and we need literature, both suitable and in abundance, that shall satisfy a *two-fold want:*

(1) *The want in the church.* What our churches need is to know what this Society is; what its principles; what its working basis; what its peculiar features, such as meet the wants of young Christians and converts and those not now Christians. Such intelligence, wisely scattered, may create a general impression that a cradle of this kind is needed in every church; and so it is.

(2) There is a want in the *Society* for increased information on any department of young people's work. We find among young people no lack of will to do, but we find what is in the church—a lacking of knowing the *how*. The literature we now

have has been of great advantage. This but proves what a power for good there would be in more of the same kind and somewhat of other kinds. The need is great of suitable and special instruction on the committee work. The story of how others do is often better than all mere theories. The story of a life is often better than preaching. It would advance the good work of this society if, in addition to tracts and leaflets full of practical hints, we had an organ—a paper to circulate in the society and outside, devoted to the interests of the organization. It might be small in size. It should be cheap except as to matter, and set upon a basis of support that it would be certain to stay. Many will read a paper who hate tracts.

It is true that literature costs something. It would throw much labor upon someone. It might make necessary the appointment and support of a General Secretary but if it is needed, *let it be done.* Five dollars from each society would pay the salary of a General Secretary, who could edit the paper, and it would also meet almost the whole expense of printing; while, in return, subscriptions and a few advertisements would help pay the expenses of the society. But what we plead for in the paper is suitable and sufficient literature.

In the short or long run, this is a question of life or death. If the society has no literature, it will fail. If it has none, the failure is deep. The existence of literature shows interest. Its increase shows that the thought and affection of men are on the service or work. Suitable and sufficient literature shows the strong and solid foundations on which we may stand, to build until our temple dome rises above the skies.

TREASURER'S REPORT.

To the Fourth Annual Conference of the Young People's Societies of Christian Endeavor:

'Your treasurer would report as follows:

CASH RECEIVED.

Balance from old account	$1 00
Society at Westerly, R. I.	2 70
Society at Monticello, Iowa	3 00
Society at Deer Isle, Me.	4 00
Pine Street Society, Portland, Me.	5 00
Central Presbyterian, Rochester, N. Y.	11 00
Society at Wellesley, Mass.	2 65
High Street Congregational Society, Auburn, Me.	2 25
Second Parish, Portland, Me.	7 00
Phillips' Church, South Boston, Mass.	20 00
Society at East Douglas, Mass.	2 35

Amount carried forward, $60 95

Amount brought forward,	$60 95
Society at Bucksport, Me.	5 00
West Congregational Church Society, Portland, Me.	4 00
Society at Plymouth, Mass.	3 70
Society at Grafton Centre, Mass.	4 35
First Baptist Society, Portland, Me.	5 50
Society at Acton, Me.	70
Society at West Taconia, Wash. Ter.	1 20
First Congregational Society, Detroit, Mich.	5 00
Howard Avenue Society, New Haven, Ct.	8 00
High Street Congregational Society, Lowell, Mass.	11 00
Society at West Newton, Mass.	5 60
Lawrence Street Society, Portland, Me.	7 00
Westminster Church Society, Rochester, N. Y.	3 00
North Avenue Church Society, North Cambridge, Mass.	5 00
Society at Lee, Mass.	10 00
North Church Society, Lynn, Mass.	10 00
Society at Newburyport, Mass.	3 00
Society at Bellville, N. J.	2 00
Society at Auburndale, Mass.	5 00
Society at St. Joseph, Mich.	4 00
Society at Conway, Mass.	3 00
Society at Chester, Vt.	1 20
Second Church Society, Denver, Col.	1 15
Society at Kennebunk, Me.	1 75
Society at Palmyra, N. Y.	1 00
Society at Boulder, Col.	3 20
Society at Wolcott, N. Y.	4 20
Society at South Egremont, Mass.	3 00
Society at Salem, Mass.	3 00
Society at Jamestown, N. Y.	3 00
Clyde Congregational Church Society, Kansas City, Mo.	1 00
Society at West Haven, Conn.	5 00
North Presbyterian Church Society, Rochester, N. Y.	6 00
John Street Congregational Church Society, Lowell, Mass.	6 40
Walnut Avenue Society, Roxbury, Mass.	8 50
Kirk Street Congregational Society, Lowell, Mass.	8 50
First Church Society, Burlington, Vt.	6 13
Amount carried forward,	$230 03

Amount brought forward,	$230	03
Society at Great Falls, N. H.	4	00
Society at Marblehead, Mass.	3	00
Immanuel Church Society, Boston, Mass.	6	50
Society at West Medford, Mass.	2	00
Society at Upton, Mass.	5	00
Society at Melrose, Mass.	10	00
Williston Society, Portland, Me.	12	28
Society at Fredonia, N. Y.	5	00
Society at Woodstock, Ill.	3	00
Society at Washington Heights, Ill.	1	00
Sale of reports and tracts	6	40
Individual subscriptions	6	50

Total $294 71

CASH PAID OUT.

J. W. Stevenson, Secretary's expenses	$13	48
Treasurer, postage and stationery	4	50
Campbell & Hanscom, printing third annual reports . . .	154	00
W. H. Pennell, printing and postage	37	39
Campbell & Hanscom, printing leaflets	18	00
James W. Stevenson, Secretary's expenses	9	49

	$236	86
Cash on hand to balance	57	85

Total $294 71

The money received from the societies as above reported was sent in response to a circular sent by the Executive Committee and a circular letter sent by the Treasurer.

The thanks of the Conference are certainly due to the societies that have so kindly responded to the call and kept the treasury supplied with sufficient funds to meet every demand.

Respectfully submitted,

W. J. VAN PATTEN.

DUTIES OF THE PRESIDENT.

The general duties of the President are clearly outlined in most, and should be in all, our Constitutions or By-Laws. The duty of presiding at all business meetings demands a clear understanding of the simpler forms of parliamentary law, that all business may be done decently and in order, and by this means our young people may incidentally gain much useful information which will avail them when they take their places in our churches and benevolent organizations. The position also calls for a perfect knowledge of the Constitution and By-Laws of the Society, that the business of the society may be confined to its legitimate channels. He should also have the faculty of preserving order in all meetings of the Society in which he may preside, that the time of the Society may not be wasted or worse than wasted by trifling and disorderly conduct, particularly among the younger members, and he should be prepared to deal kindly but firmly with those who continue to offend in this particular, either by speaking with them privately or by public reproof.

The President should, moreover, be consecrated to the work. His position demands this, and nothing less will enable him to perform the duties falling to him, sometimes called the "little duties," but not of little importance. They are real, and sometimes require more tact and patience than larger ones. He should take a personal and hearty interest in all the work of the Society, and keep informed of the work that is being done by the different committees, and to see that the committees are faithfully performing their work. He should be ready to suggest lines of work, and be ready to co-operate with them. He should be quick to discover and put in practice any good ideas of new methods of Christian work formed by individual members of the Society. In the discussions of the Society, he should studiously discourage, and, if possible, prevent, all contention, and use care to prevent subjects which may develope wide divergencies of opinion from coming before the Society at all. The Society is not a debating club, but is an organization for the developement of Christian character, and everything should be made to contribute to that end.

If there are any unpleasant duties to perform, the President should be the first to volunteer. And thus by proving that it is not his own pleasure he is seeking, but to know his Master's will, that he may do it, he will become more and more a power for good among the young people. He should remember that in the eyes of God the soul of the poorest child in the Society is of as much value as that of the wealthiest and most honored, and should receive the same care and attention. The presidency of one of our societies is not a position of honor, in the ordinary sense of the term, but a glorious opportunity for work. Let the President be like the gallant captain on the field of battle, who is ready to lead his men into the thickest of the fight. If his men are cowards, he may have to do all the fighting alone, and will, perhaps, be defeated. And someone may say: "There, I told you so; I knew he would be defeated; I always said he was too forward and self-assertive." But in all the critic may say, he will not once question the right or the necessity for the action. The point is, that in spite of all criticisms, and even though he should have to work alone, it is for the President to be faithful to his highest convictions of duty.

But let us suppose that the captain has a company of loyal men, who are ready to follow him wherever he leads. And after a fierce struggle they come off victorious; then, when the danger is over, our critic will crawl out from his safe retreat and say:

"I told you so; I knew we would win." We have in our societies a body of young people who are loyal to the truth, and who are ready to follow their leader in any work that shall weaken the power of sin and evil and strengthen the power of truth and righteousness. Let the President be more afraid of proving recreant to his trust than of the criticism of others, and think not so much of what people will say, as what *he* ought to do; and his power and influence will be increased a hundred fold. Let us rise to a sense of our responsibility, and remember these words of Paul to Timothy: "Let no man despise thy youth, but be thou an example to them that believe, in word, in manner of life, in love, in faith, in purity."

DUTIES OF THE SECRETARY.

BY MISS M. ALICE METCALF, PORTLAND, ME.

To speak of the work of a Secretary seems hardly necessary. Why, the Secretary keeps the books, writes a report of the business meetings, reads the same at the next meeting, and keeps a record of the members. "The books" implies more than one book to keep. In the first place, there is the book for the members to sign, containing the Constitution and By-Laws, and against each member's name is written his or her number of succession. [See sample sheets marked active members and associate members.] System is of the first importance, and perfecting a system, then comes to be felt the need of the Index Book, a necessary convenience, containing an alphabetical list of all members, their number, address, date of being voted into the society, and a column for remarks. This index is corrected every month by the report of the Lookout Committee. And the Lookout Committee can materially aid the Secretary by faithfully performing the duties referred to them by the Constitution, and the chairman of this committee become a sort of Assistant Secretary.

In the Record Book is kept — First, the Constitution and its amendments, also the By-Laws and the Rules. Then follows the Historical Roll, with pencil marks drawn through those names to be temporarily omitted from the Roll Call. Against each name is the succession number, the date of being voted into the Society, the date of any removal, temporary or permanent, and whatever remarks may seem to be in order, and a column for church membership. Then comes the roll of associate members, with their associate numbers, the date of being voted into the society, and the other columns for dates and remarks. When an associate is voted an active member and has signed the pledges for active membership, his or her name is erased from the associate list and entered on the active roll the same as a new member. while in the Index Book is written the new succession number and the date of admission as an active member. Then there are the honorary members, with their historical number, date of admission, date of being placed on this list, and a column for remarks, as also for other dates, if needed. Next comes the Absent List, with its many columns. In the first, the historical number; in the second, the name of the absentee; in the next, the date of admission to the society; in the next, the date when absence was granted; then, for how long; and to what place; followed by a column for remarks and for other dates. Does this seem too much for absentees? It is a good deal, but it all seems to be necessary to a large society when we consider that otherwise absentees would be practically lost to us, whereas, with the whole story in one line, each one can be supplied with new topics ·every six months, and written to if they do not report within the time specified by the By-Laws, and dropped if delinquent; thus more easily keeping clean the records and lists.   In the back of our book is a membership schedule, to be posted every month, for the month preceding, showing at a glance the admissions, changes, dismissions, etc., for each month, with the several totals for that special year, and the total from the forming of the society up to date.   There should also be a page for deceased members and pages for dismissed members, with columns for necessary dates and remarks.

The records of the business meetings follow the absent list.   It is quite necessary to record all actual business done, and to copy into its place, at the beginning of the book, any constitutional amendment, by-law or rule that may be adopted, together with its date.   Then, if new members have been voted in, to obtain their signatures as early as possible.   It has been found advisable with us to adopt a by-law requiring the signatures within two weeks after the proposed members have been accepted.   It may be necessary to officially notify such new members of their election, and here prove useful application formulas, with full name and post-office address of each applicant.

After the signing, the membership lists are posted and tickets given to the new members, admitting the holder to all the sociables, while the special tickets for friends of members are to be had of the Social Committee.   All dismissed members, honoraries, absentees, committees, sub-committees, delegates are notified as early as possible. It also falls to the lot of the Secretary to call the roll at the experience meetings.

This covers all the official business of the Secretary, unless the careful keeping of a few envelopes should be included as an official duty.   In one envelope are exchanges — copies of the Constitutions, topics, forms and pledges of other like societies — as we have received them from time to time.   In another envelope are back issues of our own Constitution, By-Laws, topics,· etc.   In another, our correspondence and cards. Probably later, as these last — particularly the letters — increase, a letter-file will be needed, but for the present the envelope is sufficient.   There is also another envelope, perhaps more a convenience than a necessity, in which is kept slips and notes till they are no longer needed for reference.

THE NEED OF A GENERAL SECRETARY.

BY REV. FRANK E. CLARK, SOUTH BOSTON, MASS.

One very patent fact concerning the Young People's Society of Christian Endeavor is, that its growth has not been forced.   In the popular phrase of the day, no one has attempted to " boom it."   As the Lord has led us on, we have tried to follow.   As He has opened one door after another, we have tried to enter in.   From the very beginning, this was true of it.   In a single church, in fearfulness and self-distrust, the work was started.   It was considered for a long time a mere experiment, until God seemed to set upon it the seal of His approval.   A single newspaper article, written without any thought of attracting special attention, was widely copied and became a living seed, which sprang up in many places. One society after another was started, at first mostly in the city and vicinity of the original society. From month to month the story went. From church to church the news spread until, in God's way and according to His place, the little one became a thousand. But of course information was desired, methods of work were inquired for, constitutions were sought. To supply this information, to answer the hundreds of letters of inquiry, became no slight task even during the first year of the life of the society. The work is growing every day; it requires more attention, more thought, more energy given to it every week. The Lord is opening the door wider and wider. Shall we enter in? Apparently we have nearly reached the limit of effort under the present system. We are fairly pushed on by Providence to the consideration of this proposition: *We need a General Secretary who shall give his whole time and effort to the work of the Society of Christian Endeavor.*

(1) And first, we need such a Secretary because the work has already outgrown the voluntary efforts of busy men. The modesty of our President may prevent him from telling you how arduous have been his labors during the past year. But I know something of what he has had to do. Together with our faithful Secretary, he has given his nights to this work oftentimes, because his days were too full of business cares and responsibilities to admit of being used. He has done what few men would have done, voluntarily and freely, out of love to God and his Master. This is a work which we cannot properly relegate much longer to voluntary efforts of a man who has his heart and his hands full of other cares. But where shall we find one unless he is appointed and paid especially for this service?

(2) In the second place, a General Secretary is needed because the work has assumed such proportions as to fill the time and task the strength of anyone who shall give himself to the work. To answer in detail the hundreds of letters which seek information; to supply the constant and increasing demand for constitutions and other literature; to address churches that desire light on this subject; to visit conferences and associations; to assist in organizing societies, is a work which may well task the strength and ability of a strong man.

(3) In the third place, we ought to have a General Secretary because the work will inevitably lag unless some such forward step is taken. God, as we believe, has put this labor upon us. He has brought us to a point where we must either advance or stand still, and standing still really means a retreat. Having reached the limit of effort under present conditions, the only chance for advance seems to be by some such appointment as we have under consideration.

(4) Fourthly and lastly, we should have a General Secretary because the time has come when such an officer can be supported. Our societies are so numerous and enthusiastic that could the matter be presented to them, there would be no difficulty in obtaining sufficient means to carry on the work. An annual contribution of ten dollars from each society, if all could be reached, would amply supply all our needs. For the first year, to be sure, it might be difficult to present the matter to the societies throughout the country, and a few of us might have to bear more than our proportional share of the expense, but we feel confident that one year of faithful effort on the part of the General Secretary would right matters and would bring a large and constantly growing constituency to his support.

And now the question comes, who shall the new Secretary be? We can answer only in general terms. He must be an *earnest, able, faithful, judicious* worker, who has no crotchets and is not a constant fault-finder; one who loves the young; one whose whole soul is devoted to Jesus Christ and His cause; and one who thoroughly and heartily believes in the Society of Christian Endeavor, its objects and aims. To install a weak, unwise or half-hearted man in such a place would be a grave mistake. The wrong Secretary would be worse than no Secretary. Better wait ten years for the right man, however the work may press upon us, than to make a mistake. But for one who is entirely consecrated, for one who thoroughly believes in our methods and aims, for one who thoroughly loves young people, I know of no grander opportunity to do the Lord's work, and to impress his influence upon the Christian life of the future, than this would afford.

Not for the sake of the Societies of Christian Endeavor would I urge the appointment of a General Secretary — the upbuilding of this organization is of minor and secondary importance. But for the sake of the young people in all our communities, for the sake of the Church of God, for the sake of the cause of the Lord Jesus Christ, I would urge this forward movement — the appointment of a General Secretary for the Young People's Society of Christian Endeavor.

THE RECORD BOOK.

SAMPLES OF ALL THE LISTS.

	Active Members. Name.	Voted into Society.	Dates.	Remarks.	Church.
1	Arthur Adams .	Feb. 5, 1883	. . . .	. . . .	Member
2	Bertram Bowers .	" " "	Apr. 6, 1885	Honorary member .	Mar. 4, 1883
3	Clara Cummings .	" " "	Jan. 19, 1885	Absentee	Member .
4	Drexel Downing	" " "	. . . . . .	. . . . . .	"

	Associate Mem. Name.	Voted Admission.	Dates.	Remarks.	Church.
1	Egbert Elwell . .	Feb. 5, 1883	Nov. 5, 1883	Active Mem. No. 97	Nov. 4, 1883
2	Florence Fenno .	" " "	. . . .	. . . . . .	. . . . .
3	George Gardner .	" " "	. . . .	. . . .	. . . .

Honorary Mem. Name.	Admitted to Society.	Voted Honorary.	Reasons for Honor.	Dates
45 Holden Harper	Feb. 5, 1883	June 2, 1884	Serving Christ in another field	.
68 Isabel Irving	Mar. 5, 1883	" "	Missionary to India	.
2 Bertram Bowers	Feb. 5, 1883	April 6, 1885	Faithfulness while in Society	.

The Absent List. Name.	Admitted to Society.	Granted Absence.	Time.	Place.	Remarks.	Dates.
57 Judson Jerrold	Feb. 5, 1883	Nov. 3, 1884	6 months	Juniatta Junction, N. J.	.	.
99 Kendall King	Nov. 5, 1883	Oct. 6, 1884	"	Kingston, Ky.	Returned	April 6, 1885
97 Egbert Elwell (1a)	Nov. 5, 1883	" "	1 year	Exeter, Eng.	.	.
3 Clara Cummings	Feb. 5, 1883	Jan. 19, 1885	6 months	Colebrook, Conn.	.	.

MEMBERSHIP SCHEDULE.
[c denotes dismissed by card.]

1883.	Active.	Associate	Honorary.	Absentees.	Dismissed.	Deceased.	Net Total.		Deceased Members. Name.	Joined Society.	Died.
Feb. 5	57	6	0	0	0	0	63	(4 a)	Leonard Lambert .	Feb. 5, 1883	May, 1884
Mar. 5	15	3	0	0	0	0	18	42	Morris Martin . . .	" "	Feb. 11, '85
Apr. 2	11	5	0	0	0	0	16				
May 7	7	1	0	0	0	0	8				

	Dismissed Members. Name.	Voted Admission.	Voted Dismission.	Causes and Remarks.	Dates.
149	Nelson Norris	May 5, 1884	Nov. 3, 1884	Non-attendance and non-conformance to rules	
46	Oliver Osgood . .	Feb. 5, 1883	Nov. 3, 1884	Card to Oberlin Y. P. S. C. E.	
93	Parker Price. New No. 172	Oct. 1, 1883	Dec. 1, 1884	Non-attendance, etc. Readmitted	Mar. 2, 1885
117	Rose Robbins	Jan. 14, 1884	June 2, 1885	" "	

THE INDEX BOOK.

SAMPLE PAGE IN LETTER G.

	Name.	Residence.	Voted into Society.	Remarks	Dates.
3	Gardner, George .	25 Grove St. .	Feb. 5, 1883	. . .	. . . . .
94	Gerrish, Grace . .	17 Green St. .	Oct. 1, 1883	. . .	. . . . .
91	Gerrish, Grant . .	" " "	June 4, 1883	. . .	. . . . .
115	Gifford, Greeley . .	99 Gresham St.	Jan. 14, 1884	. . .	. . . . .
92	Gifford, Glen . . .	" " "	June 4, 1883	Excluded	June 2, 1885
75	Gravesend, Gerald	64 " "	Apr. 2, 1883	. . . .	. . . .
76	Gravesend, Gertrude	" " "	" " "	. . .	. . . .

G H I J K L M N O P Q R S T U V W Y

THE FUTURE OF THE SOCIETY.

BY REV. J. L. HILL, LYNN, MASS.

There is undoubtedly an element in this movement which is unique, and which is certain to give it a lasting place in all successful church administration, and that is, its provision that every young disciple shall, like young Timothy, "exercise himself unto godliness." Mr. A. T. Stewart was fond of calling his store a school for training young men in business. They learned to sell by selling. They were taught how to do things by doing them. One must get the pronunciation of a language by speaking it. In an arithmetic, there is a simple statement of the principle, and then follow the exercises. Christianity is more than a science; it is an art. This latter is acquired by practice, chiefly. Young men and women can be trained for the church work of committees by putting them upon committees. Young persons can best learn church polity by becoming a part of the church machinery, and studying its working from within the work.

A movement has begun at both the East and West to found what is denominated a school for Christian workers. One of its three objects, specified in its prospectus and upon its letter-heads, is to train persons to become helpers to pastors. If all the churches of Christendom were together in convention, a vote could be passed unanimously, that such training would better begin young. "When older persons are converted," said Mr. Shauffler, "I only aspire barely to get them ready for the Kingdom of Heaven. When, however, younger persons are converted, I see in them the possibility of becoming Christian workers."

A demand from ministerial sources for relief and assistance is springing up, such as the church has never known before. A day or two in every week is spent by overworked pastors in attention to details and in routine duties that could be relegated in part to swifter feet and to fresher lives, and that with mutual benefit. After an understanding had been reached and an affectionate confidence established, I doubt not that every pastor who has much of a care could hand to a committee at its weekly meeting a memorandum — not insignificant — of steps to be taken, kindly deeds to be done, and immediate work to be accomplished. Most churches cannot employ a pastor's assistant. It is better for the young workers that this should not be done. *Work* has incalculable worth to the worker. "I like your work," said a sagacious observer, "for what it does for the man who takes hold of it. At first, that young man had barely religion enough to save him, and now he carries fire and enthusiasm into all our gatherings for prayer."

Beside the desire that the societies represented in this convention consider our obligation to become helpers of pastors, there is another matter which ought to be regarded in our future work. It has become a matter of common repute that in the membership of our churches, women outnumber men in a proportion of two to one. I see it stated that this is the exact proportion in the denomination with which I am most familiar, taking the United States together. In New England, it must be confessed that the women outnumber men in even a larger proportion. Now, my observation and experience make me ready to affirm that the Society of Christian Endeavor can be greatly useful in correcting this anomalous condition. For a time church growth stood mocking us afar off. The provision for the wants of young people was altogether too scant. We lacked a *little* chariot suitable for working a pony team.

Being unattached, they are running wild, finding their own pasture. As much as it is to be deplored, in too many instances boys graduate from the Sunday School. As a matter of fact, they fall down and out between the Sunday School and the church. That is the hiatus which this organization is designed to bridge. Hitherto we have gathered great multitudes of fishes only to lose them again. There has been a wide hole in the net. We should have commended ourselves as wiser fishers of men if, like the early disciples, we had sooner pulled up to shore and mended our nets. Since the organization of our Society, five-sixths of the male members who have joined our church have come from the Society's ranks. Now, Mr. President, in the future of our work, we owe it to the churches to get a hold on boys, to introduce them, young, into our work, to interest them, and develope them, and Christianize them, that they may become pillars in the temple of our God.

The desirability of this form of accession leads me to suggest a grave danger that has already begun to menace the future of our Society. It is the tendency of those who are already members to make a social set. There is a fellowship, and it is delightful to witness, and the danger is, that it may become a "ring." The danger is, that our organization shall become like the sewing society in the church. Certain ladies constitute it. If other ladies had composed it from the beginning, they would have been it. There is no reason at all why other ladies should not be the sewing society as well as those that compose it. So with our societies. Social congenialities begin to threaten us. The danger increases as time goes on. Nothing will limit our growth like a clique. Many a society, once designed for all, has struck on that rock. Some churches even get wrecked on the same. A society with a clique in it, has taken the oars up into the boat and has begun to drift.

There is another inevitable incident to the future of the Society which now needs expression and discussion. If this organization be a *school* for the training of Christian workers, how can we form what — to keep the figure — would be an *alumni association.* I maintain, first, that no delinquent active member ought ever to be relegated, because of delinquency, to the associate list. That degrades it. It makes a motley company. It comes to consist of the ring-streaked and speckled. The roll of associate membership becomes thus a black list. There is nothing necessarily opprobrious about associate membership. It is a part of our working machinery. We must reserve that rank for those of good repute. It makes a difference, if a man stands at a threshold, whether he is facing in or facing out. Furthermore, it is not the place to carry the names of those who have removed from town or have grown too old to be advantageously used in the working force of a *Young People's* Society of Christian Endeavor. We must have, then, in our future work, what, for want of a name, I will call the Rank of Honorary Membership, or Affiliated Membership, to which Active Members, for various good reasons, may be retired.

Such provision must be made that Societies of Christian Endeavor shall be composed, chiefly, always, of young persons, as is contemplated in its name, else, as we who compose its working force shall grow old together, we shall carry the Society over into a membership of the middle-aged and even of the hoary-headed.

A BUSINESS VIEW OF WAYS AND MEANS.

BY W. J. VAN PATTEN, OF BURLINGTON, VT.

Our earnest desire is to enlarge the influence and extend the work of the Young People's Societies of Christian Endeavor. What are the ways which seem to be open to us through which we may accomplish this end? What are the means which we may employ? In the first place, there are the ways already used with such manifestly blessed results. The principal one has been individual effort—voluntary, persistent, enthusiastic—the best way of all in which a good work can be carried on; the way in which the heart and the mind and the will are put into it, and which makes it sure of that success, with God's help (who never fails such a worker), which secures the best and most lasting results. The continuance of this individual effort in extending the work is most greatly to be desired. We must not allow ourselves to think that we can invent any organized or machine methods that will take its place.

The next most important work that has been done is the printing and circulating of books, proceedings and circulars. This method of spreading information must be continued. The necessity of it is apparent to all. The question is, how can it be done so as to be the most nearly self-supporting? I would suggest that the more expensive pamphlets and books have a price fixed upon them which will cover the cost, and that societies and individuals be furnished as they may desire, at these prices. I think many societies would be glad to avail themselves of reports and other printed matter if they understood that they could be obtained for a small sum which is barely the cost of printing. A very useful book could be compiled from the proceedings of the conferences thus far held, on the work of the various committees and the best methods   securing the fulfilment of the obligations resting upon members. A great many societies feel that they need help along those lines. We shall, however, need other printing that we may scatter widely and without price. This is one of the ways for which means must be devised by this conference. One of the things I would suggest in this connection is the publication, in cheap form, on light paper, without covers, of the minutes of this conference, without the papers. I wish it might be sent to every pastor and Sunday School Superintendent in the land. Surely nothing would do more to awaken a spirit of inquiry into the methods and objects of the Society. Further supplies will also be necessary of the circulars and leaflets already issued by the Executive Committee, and which have heretofore proven so useful.

The holding of state and local conferences is another way which has been already used, and which should be promoted and encouraged. I hope the coming year such conferences will be greatly multiplied and that they will not be confined to churches that already have Christian Endeavor Societies formed, but that all young people's societies be invited to participate, and representatives from churches as well, to the end that they may become acquainted with our work and aims. There are ways which can plainly be seen to be necessary in the future. What more is necessary or advisable?

Before projecting any new plans, let us look over our field and note the extent and character of it, and what may be the necessity of pushing on in this one particular line of Christian effort. The world, in a certain large sense, is the field of this organization. It should, at least, be able and ready to lend a helping hand to any, whoever they are, wherever they may be, who may desire to try our plans and methods. But more particularly are our plans needed in our own country. Comparatively few of the churches or ministers even yet know what they are, or the advantage there would come from an alliance of their young people with the great number of earnest young Christians that are banded together in these societies. Then we can at present only expect to gain the attention of such evangelical denominations as usually co-operate in Christian work. This, then, is our immediate field — our own country, and the portion of the field which we can work is that occupied by the denominations indicated. Whatever new plans are proposed should be such as can be used through the whole extent of this home field.

Two of the most important new ways have already been discussed before this conference. The establishment of a paper which shall be a means of communication between the societies, and also a guide and help, is one of the things most greatly needed. I firmly believe its good effects would be great and immediate. The employment of a Secretary has been shown to be another way which is very important. This, if done, will require considerable funds to provide for salary, travelling and incidental expenses.

Another way in which I believe the work could be advanced is, to have arrangements made so that these societies could be represented before the county, state and national meetings of the different denominations, by men of ability and influence who by trial know the value of the work. There are many opportunities of this kind when they would be glad to hear, perhaps, not so much of theory, but of the actual work done. And I doubt not that there are plenty of men who, if called on, would gladly respond. It might be necessary, in some cases, to pay their expenses, but, on the whole, the cost would be very little for the good that would be done. It would involve considerable labor in correspondence to arrange details, and perhaps cannot be fully carried out until we have a Secretary. These, then, are the ways in which we are to endeavor to carry forward the work of the societies, seeking to increase their number and to add to the efficiency of all.

In speaking now of the means which we shall need, we shall consider only the subject of financial means. The work which we desire to do will necessitate the use of considerable money, and the question now before us is, how is our Executive Committee to obtain it? There are two methods by which money has been raised in the past: First, by pledges of the societies represented in the conference, given at one of the meetings; second, by the solicitation of subscriptions from all societies. By this latter method, about $300 were obtained the past year. It is plain, from our past experience, that some more effective method must be devised in order to raise the funds needed to carry out the plans which are proposed, and which seem so necessary. There are four sources to which we may look for the help we need. These four are individuals, societies, churches, and the annual and life memberships as proposed. We must ask individual Christians who have seen and who appreciate our work to aid us in pushing it forward. If we can obtain a constituency of such as will make this one of the causes to which they give regularly and systematically, as unto the Lord, the question of finances will be solved. How can this be brought about? The first thing will be, to obtain from local societies a list of persons to whom we may properly, and with hope of success, appeal; persons who already know something of the purposes and results of our work, and who believe in it. Circular letters could then be prepared and sent to such persons, through some member of the local society, and their subscriptions solicited. This plan, judiciously carried out, would, I doubt not, bring a generous response. Individuals can also be solicited by personal appeal from any that desire to further this work. In regard to help from societies, I do not know that I have any new suggestions to make. I would recommend that both the ways heretofore used be employed again. Let us ask the delegates in attendance here to pledge such sums as they feel are right, on behalf of their societies. Then let all other societies, whenever established, be asked to help on the good work, and responses will come, as last year, from Kennebunk to Tacoma; from where the sun first looks upon the rocky shores of Maine, as it rises from the bosom of the Atlantic, to where it bids good-night to this fair land of ours, as it sinks into the Pacific.

The third source to which we may look for help is the churches. There are few, if any, of the benevolent objects to which our churches contribute which so closely concern them, and from which they may so surely and quickly expect dividends of good results. There is no reason, then, why we should not ask for help in this direction. I doubt not there are many pastors who will gladly bring the matter before their churches, and ask for us their aid. With these plans carried out, we can hope and expect to receive whatever means may be necessary to the carrying out of wise and needed ways, for, as has been said before, " no Christian work for the young, when rightly presented to Christian people, ever suffered for lack of means." Let us, then, take up with good heart whatever work seems necessary and right, with full faith that the blessing of Him for whom we labor will be upon it.

BY-LAWS OF THE UNITED SOCIETY OF CHRISTIAN ENDEAVOR.

ARTICLE I.

Any person may become a member of this corporation by a two-thirds vote of those present at any meeting.

ARTICLE II.

Each member shall pay an annual fee of one dollar. Any member failing to pay the annual fee within six months after notice, their membership shall lapse.

ARTICLE III.

Any member paying twenty dollars at any one time shall be entitled to life membership, and shall not be required to pay any annual fee.

ARTICLE IV.

The officers of this corporation shall be a Chairman, Secretary, Treasurer, Auditor and Board of Trustees consisting of eleven members, of which number the Chairman, Secretary and Treasurer shall be members, ex-officio; all of whom shall be members in good standing of evangelical churches, and shall be elected by ballot.

ARTICLE V.

Eight members of the Board of Trustees shall be elected at the first meeting, of whom two shall hold office for four years, two for three years. two for two years, and two for one year. The Chairman, Secretary, Treasurer, Auditor, and two members of the Board of Trustees shall be elected annually, and the two members of the Board of Trustees shall hold office for four years.

ARTICLE VI.

The Chairman, when present, shall preside at all meetings of the corporation and Board of Trustees, and in his absence the Secretary shall call the meeting to order, and a Chairman pro tem. be chosen by ballot.

ARTICLE VII.

It shall be the duty of the Secretary to keep a correct record of each meeting, notify all officers and committees of their election and appointment, serve as secretary of the Board of Trustees, and give seasonable notice of all meetings.

ARTICLE VIII.

The Treasurer shall collect the annual fees, donations and income accruing to the corporation, and shall pay the orders of the Trustees or their committees. He shall, at the annual meeting, exhibit to the corporation an account of his receipts and payments, and a statement of the funds and property of the corporation; and he shall give bond in such sum and with such sureties as the Trustees shall direct, for the faithful discharge of his duty, and the payment and delivery of all the property of the corporation in his hands to his successor in office. He shall also present a statement of the condition of the Treasury to the Trustees when requested.

ARTICLE IX.

It shall be the duty of the Auditor to examine carefully and compare the books, securities, vouchers and financial report of the Treasurer previous to the annual meeting, and at any other time when directed, and make report on the same to the corporation.

ARTICLE X.

The Trustees, four of whom shall constitute a quorum, shall meet at least once every three months, and as much oftener as they think proper. It shall be their duty to manage the funds of the corporation, to solicit aid for the organization, and generally to do what they think best to carry its designs into effect; and in order to facilitate their business, they may, for the purposes aforesaid, appoint a committee or committees, and any other subordinate officers which they may deem necessary, and make such by-laws for their government as they may deem expedient; and they shall make report of their proceedings at every annual meeting.

ARTICLE XI.

There shall be an annual meeting of this corporation at such place in the State of Maine as the Trustees shall appoint, in the month of July or August, notice of which meeting shall be sent by mail, by the Secretary, to each member at least two weeks before the time for holding said meeting.

ARTICLE XII.

Seven members of this corporation shall constitute a quorum at all meetings.

ARTICLE XIII.

Special meetings of the corporation may be called whenever the trustees or any ten members of the corporation shall deem it necessary, in which case application shall be made to the Chairman or Secretary, either of whom, when thus applied to, shall notify the same at such time and place as such officer shall designate, notice of such meeting to be given in the manner prescribed for annual meeting.

ARTICLE XIV.

In case of vacancy in any of the offices, by death, resignation or otherwise, the Trustees shall have power to fill the same.

ARTICLE XV.

Any of the foregoing articles may be repealed, added to, or amended at any annual meeting on a vote of two-thirds of the members present, or at any special meeting, when notice of the same shall have been given in the call for said meeting.

www.ingramcontent.com/pod-product-compliance
Lightning Source LLC
Chambersburg PA
CBHW020517030426
42337CB00011B/425